THE THREEFOLD
SOCIAL ORDER

THE THREEFOLD
SOCIAL ORDER

By
Rudolf Steiner

ANTHROPOSOPHIC PRESS, INC.
New York

This work, formerly published with the title,
The Threefold Commonwealth, is a revised translation of *Die Kernpunkte der sozialen Frage* (Vol. 23
in the Bibliographic Survey, 1961). Revised and
rendered into English by Frederick C. Heckel.

Second edition, 1972

Library of Congress Catalog Card No. 66–29676

This translation has been authorized for the
Western Hemisphere by agreement with the
Rudolf Steiner Nachlassverwaltung, Dornach,
Switzerland.

Printed in the United States of America

TABLE OF CONTENTS

TRANSLATOR'S PREFACE

The purpose of this translation, a free rendering, is to make available to the American reader the essence of a book that describes a sound social order and the means by which it can be achieved. It is as timely today as when it was published in 1919 in German. The original English translation is now out of print. The problems of society have intensified but their basic pattern has, as Rudolf Steiner predicted, remained the same.

Considering that the work was not something intellectually thought out but arrived at by a penetrating study of what still works in the inner depths of society and of the men striving for social change, its continuing validity is perhaps not surprising. Steiner, of course, was addressing himself to European social thinkers, always more interested in an "ideological" approach than the American, who is primarily a doer. Even European socialists have come to think far less in terms of ideologies today than used to be the case. In Germany there has been a departure from the principle of nationalization of industry, and this is true to a large extent in Great Britain also.

One might say that ideologies have, everywhere, given way to pragmatism. If Steiner were to write this book today he would describe economic conditions as they have developed after World War II, and still come to the same basic conclusions. In close contact with many of the men involved, he was in a position that made possible both external study of the social phenomena and a penetration into the realities behind them. For the latter he could use the methods of approach presented in his philosophical world conception.

The effort here has been, besides omitting topical material no longer of such immediate interest, to break up the original lengthy sentence structure that is appropriate in the German language. Dr. Steiner himself said that if he had been writing this book for England and America he would have written it quite differently. For students of history interested in details concerning the break-up of the German and Austrian Empires, important background facts related to that time are available in the original German work, *Die Kernpunkte der socialen Frage.* For this and other omissions from the text, the undersigned takes full responsibility.

Special thanks are due to Lisa D. Monges, who corrected certain errors in the original English translation, and to S. J. Kingsley, E. Hinternhoff and H. Mehrtens, for their editorial help with the entire text or portions of it.

Frederick C. Heckel

Threefold Farm
Spring Valley, N. Y.
August, 1966

FOREWORD AS TO THE PURPOSE OF THIS BOOK

We are confronted by demands for social reconstruction. These pose grave problems with far-reaching implications. This book is written with the conviction that their solution must be looked for along lines not yet considered. Its aim is to show what has to be done in order that social demands coming from a large part of mankind may be turned in the direction of conscious social purpose.

Welcome or unwelcome, the facts of social life are present and must be reckoned with. Those who may object to the author's way of discussing proletarian demands should bear this in mind. He wants to present life as it really is. He is aware of the fatal consequences that will result if people refuse to look at the facts. These facts have arisen out of the life of modern mankind.

The so-called experts may not be pleased by this approach, which they may feel is not practical. It is their approach, however, that has led to the situation from which mankind is suffering today. They may condemn this book at the start because its opening pages deal less with the economic life than with the spiritual-cultural life of modern mankind. Yet it is the author's conviction, based on experience, that unless people pay close attention to the spiritual-cultural life of today they will continue to add fresh mistakes to the old ones.

On the other hand, what is said here will not altogether please those people who keep repeating that man must rise above absorption in purely material interests, that he must turn to "ideals," to the things of the "spirit." The author recognizes only that spirituality which forms the substance of man's own life. It shows its power just as much in mastering the problems of practical life as it does in constructing a philosophy that is able to satisfy the needs of man's soul.

The important point is not the knowledge (or supposed knowledge) of a spiritual life, but rather that the spiritual life enables man to grasp realities. The author's point of view may be of special use since he avoids any aloofness from life.

The social question discussed in this book concerns economic life, the rights of men, and the spiritual-cultural life. The author endeavors to show how the true form of the social question emerges as an outcome of the requirements of these three aspects of social life.

Only through a perception of this can the impulses come that make it possible to give these three branches of social life a shape that can lead to health within the social order. In earlier stages of mankind's evolution there were social instincts holding these three branches together in a way adapted to the human nature of that period. At present man is faced with the necessity of working out this combination of functions through conscious social will and purpose.

In those countries where the question of a social purpose is most pressing we find an overlapping and interplay of old instincts and new consciousness. The results of this are quite inadequate for the needs of modern mankind. A great deal of social thinking today is neither clear-sighted nor conscious, because the old instincts are still at work. They weaken men's capacity for understanding and dealing with urgent facts.

In the author's opinion it is necessary to recognize this fully before it is possible to apprehend the forms that the industrial economy, the rights of man and the spiritual-cultural life must take to conform to the demands of the modern age. The following pages indicate the lines that these new forms must inevitably follow. It is a path leading to social ends in keeping with the actual realities and urgent needs of life. The author believes that only through effort in this direction can our social will and purpose surmount mere utopianism and wordy sentiment.

If anyone still thinks this book has a somewhat utopian character he should consider the pictures people draw in their own minds of the kind of society they seek, and how far from life such pictures are. That is the very reason why these people, when they meet with something drawn from reality and experience, look at it as utopian. To many, nothing is "concrete" that is outside their own customary line of thought. So the concrete itself is an abstraction to them if it is something about which they are not accustomed to think.* Therefore, they will think this book is abstract.

---

* April, 1919. The author has, in the pages which follow, deliberately avoided confining himself to the terms in common use in standard treatises on political economy. He knows quite well the places which a technical economist will pick out as being amateurish. But he has chosen his mode of expression partly because he wishes to address himself *also* to people who are not familiar with the literature of sociology and economics. But he has done this chiefly because, in his opinion, most of what is peculiarly technical in such writings will be shown by a new age to be incomplete and defective, even in the very form of its expression.

It may also be thought that some reference should have been made to other persons whose social ideas bear an incidental resemblance to the author's own. But it must be remembered that in the whole conception presented here, one which the author believes he owes to long years of practical experience, the essential point is not whether a particular thought has taken this or that form. The starting point is the important thing, and the road one takes in giving

With people whose minds are harnessed to a party program the author's views will also, at first, find no favor. He is well aware of this. But he believes that it will not be long before many party men come to the conclusion that the actual facts of evolution have gone far beyond the programs of their parties. They will see the urgent necessity of freeing themselves from all such party programs and forming an independent opinion.

practical realization to the impulses that underlie this conception. As may be seen from Chapter IV, the author was already doing what he could to implement these ideas in actual practice at a time when ideas that seem somewhat similar had not as yet attracted any attention.

PREFACE TO THE NEW EDITION OF 1920

Anyone approaching the social problems confronting us, with utopian ideas, is by that very fact rendered incapable of understanding these problems. Personal views and feelings as to the value of particular solutions are likely to lead a person astray. This would be true even with a perfect theoretical solution that someone might try to press upon his fellow men. It is simply because public life can no longer be affected in such a way. Men today are so constituted that they could never say, "Here is somebody who understands the social institutions that are needed. We will take his opinion and act on it."

Ideas about social life cannot be brought home to people in such a fashion. That fact is fully recognized in this book, already known to a fairly large public. Those who have set it down as utopian have missed its aim and intention altogether. Such judgments have come especially from people who personally cling to a utopian form of thought. There are many of that sort, particularly in the field of economics, and their prevalence points to an important fact, namely, the remoteness of people's thoughts from real life. This is a grave matter because with such a mode of thought one cannot hope to master the intricacies of the social problem.

Modern man has evolved a spiritual-cultural life that is to a great degree dependent on state institutions and on economic forces. While still a child, the human being is brought under the education of the state. Furthermore, he can be educated only in the way permitted by the industrial and economic conditions of his environment.

One might easily think that this would result in a person's being well qualified for present-day conditions. One could believe that the state can arrange education (the essence of the spiritual-cultural side of public life) in the best interests of the human community. Further, one might suppose that to educate people to fill available jobs in their environment was the best thing that could be done both for them and for society.

It devolves upon this book, an unpopular task, to show that the chaotic condition of our public life comes from the dependence of the spiritual-cultural life on the state and on industrial economy, and further, that the setting free of spiritual life from this dependence is one part of the burning social question.

This involves attacking wide-spread errors. For a long time people have thought of State Education as benefiting human progress, and socialistically-minded people find it hard to conceive of society not educating the individual to its service, according to its own standards. It is hard to recognize that a thing that was all right at an earlier period of history may later become all wrong. After the Middle Ages it had been necessary for the state to take over the control of education from those circles which had had exclusive possession of it. But to continue this arrangement is a grave social mistake.

This is the content of the first part of the book. The spiritual life did mature to freedom within the framework of the state. But it cannot now rightly enjoy and exercise this freedom unless it is granted self-government. It must become a completely independent branch of the body social, with the educational system under the management of those who are actually engaged in the teaching. There should be no interference from the state or industry.

The objection will be raised that even under such a self-governing spiritual life things will not be perfect. But in real life such a thing as perfection is not to be expected. All one can aim for is the best that is possible.

The new abilities that children bring with them will really pass into the life of the community when their care rests entirely with people who can judge and decide educational questions on spiritual-cultural grounds alone. From such a system the state and the economic life can receive the forces they need, forces they cannot receive when they themselves shape spiritual life from their own points of view. Thus the directors of a free spiritual life should also have the responsibility for such things as law schools, trade schools and technical colleges.

The principles expressed in this book are bound to arouse many prejudices. But basically these come from the unconscious conviction that people connected with education must necessarily be impractical and remote from life. People who think in this way do not see that it is just when educators cannot arrange their lines of work themselves that they become impractical. Our anti-social conditions are brought about because people are turned out into social life without having been educated to feel socially. They have been brought up and trained by persons who themselves have been made strangers to real life by having their work laid down from outside.

This book will also rouse all sorts of questions in utopian minds. Artists and other spiritual workers will anxiously ask whether genius will find itself better off in the free spiritual life than in the one that the state and the economic powers are providing at present. They should remember that this book is not intended to be utopian; it never lays down a hard-and-fast theory. It never says this or that must be done this way or that. It aims to promote forms of social life that, from their joint working, will lead to desirable conditions. Anyone judging life from experience rather than prejudices based on theory will say, "When there is a free spiritual community that provides its own guidance, anyone who is creating out of his own genius will have a prospect of his work being duly appreciated."

The "social question" is not something that has just cropped up, nor can it be solved by any handful of people or a parliament—and stay solved. It is a part of our recent civilization and it has come to stay. It will have to be solved over again for each moment of the world's historical evolution. This is because man's life has entered on a phase in which something that starts by being a social institution turns again and again into something anti-social, and has in turn to be reconstructed.

A human or animal body, having been fed and satisfied, passes again into a state of hunger. Likewise does the body social go from a state of order again into disorder. There is no universal remedy for social conditions any more than there is a food that will permanently satisfy the body. But men can enter into forms of social community which, through their joint action will bring man's existence constantly back into the social path. One of these is the self-governing spiritual-cultural branch of the body social.

Everything going on at the present time makes two social needs obvious: free self-administration for the spiritual-cultural life, and for the economic life, associative labor. The modern industrial economy is made up of the production, circulation and consumption of commodities. These are the processes for satisfying human wants, and in these processes human beings and their activities are involved.

Everyone has a part interest in these processes and must share in them as far as he is able. It is only the individual himself who can know and feel what he actually needs. Depending on his insight into the inter-acting life of the whole, he will judge as to what he himself should accomplish. This was not always so, nor is it so all over the world even today, but it is mainly the case among the civilized portion of mankind.

Economic evolution has kept enlarging its circles. The once self-contained household economy developed into a town economy, and this into a state economy. Today we stand before world economy. While the old does of course linger on, these sequences are essentially true.

It is completely useless to aim at organizing the economic forces into an abstract world community. Private economic organizations have, to a very large extent, become merged in state economic organizations. But the state communities were created by forces other than the purely economic, and the effort to transform the state communities into economic communities is what has brought about the social chaos of these recent times.

Economic life is struggling to take the form its own peculiar forces give it, independent of state institutions and of political lines of thought. The only way this form can be realized is through the growth of Associations that spring up out of purely economic considerations. These will include consumers, traders and producers. Their size and scope will be regulated by the actual conditions of life. Those too small would show themselves to be too expensive to operate. Those too large would get beyond the economic grasp of management.

Practical needs, as they come up, will show each Association the best way of establishing connections with the others. People having to move from one place to another will not be hampered in any way by Associations of this kind. They will find it quite easy to move from one group to another when their management is economic and not political. Also, one can conceive possible arrangements within such an associative system that would work with the facility of a money-circulation.

Within the individual Associations a general harmony of interests can prevail, provided there is practical sense and technical knowledge. The regulation of the production, circulation and consumption of goods will not be done by laws, but by the persons concerned, out of their own direct insight and interests. The necessary insight will be developed through people's own share in the life of the Associations, and the fact that the various interests are obliged to arrive at a mutual balance by contract, will guarantee that the goods circulate at their proper relative values.

This sort of economic combination by agreement is not the same as that which exists in the modern labor unions. These are active in the economic field, but they are based on political models. They are political bodies where people debate rather than meet to consider the economic aspects of things and agree on the services to be reciprocally rendered.

In these Associations there will not be the "wage earners" sitting, using their power to get the highest possible wages out of the employers. There will be the manual workers, cooperating with the spiritual workers who direct production, and with those interested as consumers. The mutual aim will be a balance between one form of service and another, brought about through an adjustment of prices.

Beware of thinking that this can be done by general debate in parliamentary assemblies. Who would ever be at work if an endless number of people had to spend their time negotiating about the work?

Everything will take place by agreement between people and between Associations, while production continues. The necessary requirement is that the joint agreement be in accordance with the insight of the workers and the interests of the consumers.

Saying this is not describing any Utopia. For there is no particular way laid down in which this or that question must be settled. One is only pointing out how people will settle matters for themselves, once they start working in forms of community that are in accordance with their special insights and interests.

Two things work to bring men together into such communities. One of them is human nature, which gives men their wants and needs. The other is a free spiritual life. This will develop the necessary insight in people. Anyone who thinks realistically will admit that associative communities of this kind can spring up at any time. What hinders this development is the notion of "organizing" industrial and economic life from outside. The kind of economic organization discussed here rests on voluntary, free association, and derives its pattern from the combined common sense of each individual.

If the "haves" and the "have-nots" are together in one organization, it will be found, if no non-economic forces intervene, that the "haves" are obliged to render the "have-nots" service for service.

While in the free spiritual life only those forces inherent in this life itself will be at work, the only values that count in an associative economic life will be the economic ones that grow up under the Associations. The individual's part in economic life will become clear to him from living and working along with his economic associates, and the weight he carries in the economic system will be in exact proportion to the service he renders within it.

How those who are unfitted to render service will find their place in the general economy, is discussed later in this book.

Thus the body social falls into two independent branches, able to afford each other mutual support owing to the fact that each has its own administration and management. Between these two must come a third. This is the true "state" branch of the body social. Here all those things find a place that depend on the combined judgment and feelings of every person of voting age.

In the free spiritual-cultural life, everyone is active in line with his special abilities. In the economic, each person fills the place that falls to him as a result of his connection with the rest of the associative network. In the political state-life of rights, each comes into his own as a human being. He stands on his simple human value. This has nothing to do with his abilities in the free spiritual life and is independent, too, of whatever value the associative economic system may set on the goods he produces.

Hours of labor and working conditions are shown in this book to be matters for the political rights life, for the state. Here everyone meets on an equal footing, because the activities and functions of control are limited to fields in which all men alike are competent to form an opinion. This is the branch of the body social where men's rights and duties are adjusted.

The unity of the body social will come into being out of the separate, free expansion of its three functions. In the course of this book it is shown what form the energies of capital and of the means of production as well as the use of land can take under the joint action of these three functions of the social organism.

The book was first published in April, 1919. Since then I have presented a series of explanatory articles, now in a separate volume.*

The ideas in this book have been won from the observation of life. It is out of the observation of actual life that they ask to be understood.

---

* *In Elaboration of the Threefold Commonwealth.*

THE THREEFOLD
SOCIAL ORDER

CHAPTER I

THE NATURE OF THE SOCIAL QUESTION
IN THE LIFE OF MODERN MAN

The great catastrophe of the War (World War I) reveals how inadequate was men's thinking concerning the social problem. They imagined that they understood what the worker really wants. The demands of the workers, formerly suppressed, are coming to the surface as the powers instrumental in their suppression are now in part destroyed. In many parts of the world, leaders have failed completely to understand the indestructible nature of these human impulses.

The greatest illusions existed among certain key people who, in 1914, could have checked the rush into this war. These persons actually believed that a military victory for their side would hush the mutterings of impending social storm. They have since recognized that it was their own attitude and its consequences that first brought these tendencies to life. During these last fateful years, these leading individuals and the leading classes have been obliged to attune their behavior to the demands of the Socialists. If they could have disregarded this group, they would often have been glad to act differently. The effects of all this are seen in the form events are taking today.

The facts are now before us, fully ripe, and yet the thoughts that accompanied their development are no match for them. While hoping that current happenings could serve the social ideals people had in mind, men have found themselves practically powerless to solve the problems.

The opinion of those under the delusion that it would be possible to retain the old scheme of things in the face of the demands of the workers must be dismissed. When we look at the aims of those who want to remodel social life, we have to admit that party programs are drifting about among us like the dried corpses of now dead creeds. The facts call for decisions for which the creeds of the old parties are altogether unprepared. The parties certainly did evolve along with the facts, but they and their habits of thought have not kept pace with events.

The tragedy revealed in all the attempts to solve the social question arises because the real meaning of the working-class struggle has been misunderstood. Men by no means always read their own purposes correctly.

What is the real meaning of the modern working-class movement? What is its will? Does the usual thinking about the "social problem" reveal that question in its true form? Or is an altogether different line of thought needed?

Such questions cannot be approached impartially unless one has had the opportunity of coming into intimate relationship with the modern worker's soul, his feeling-life. Much has been said and written about how the developments of recent economic life have led to the current demands of the workers. True enough, these have been evolved during the growth period of modern science and capitalism. But recognition of this fact gives no clue at all to the impulses behind these demands. The fact is that, although the demands are economic, the underlying impulses are of a purely human character. One must arrive at the cause of these impulses if one would understand the true form of the social question.

There is a word of striking significance frequently used by the modern worker: he has become "class-conscious." He no longer follows, more or less unconsciously, the lead of the other classes. He knows he is a member of a class apart and is determined that the relation established between his class and the other classes shall be turned to good account for his own interests.

The way this word, "class-conscious," is used by the worker standing in the midst of modern technical industry and capitalism, gives an important clue to his view of life. His soul has been impressed and fired by scientific teachings about economic life and its bearing on the destinies of men, and the idea that the "uneducated" working man has had his head turned by Marxism and by later labor writers of the Marxist school will not help towards the necessary understanding of the true facts.

The scientific evolution of recent times is responsible for the concepts that fill the consciousness of the working man. In the demands put forward by the workers today, whether moderates or radicals, we have the expression, not of economic life somehow metamorphosed into human impulse, but of economic science by which the working-class consciousness is possessed. This stands out clearly in the literature of the labor movement, with its scientific flavor and journalistic style.

The individual, working at his machine, may be a complete stranger to "science." Yet those who enlighten him as to his own position borrow their method from this same "science."

Everything said about modern economic life, the machine age and capitalism, may throw an instructive light on the underlying facts of the modern working class movement. But the decisive light on the present social situation does not come directly from the fact that the worker has been placed at the machine and harnessed to the capitalist scheme of things. This light comes from the different fact that his class consciousness has been filled with a definite kind of thought, shaped at the machine under the influence of the capitalist economy.

Many people may look at the stress laid on this factor as a mere dialectic play upon terms, but anyone who wants to understand the working-class movement must start by knowing how the worker thinks. For the working-class movement, all the way from its moderate efforts at reform to its most devastating excesses, is not created by "forces outside man," that is to say "economic impulses." This movement is created by human beings, their mental conceptions and the impulses of their will. These human ideas and impulses do not lie in what capitalism and the machine have implanted in the worker's consciousness. The labor movement turned to modern science for the sources of its thought because capitalism and the machine could give to the soul of the worker no nourishment worthy of a human being.

The medieval craftsman did not feel this lack. He got such inner substance from his craft that his humanity was enhanced by his work. Tending a machine under the capitalist scheme of things, the man was thrown back upon himself, his own inner life. As a result, the worker's class consciousness turned towards the scientific type of thought.

This change occurred at the time the leading classes were working towards a scientific mode of thought which, however, was lacking in spiritual force. The old views of the universe gave man his place as a soul in the total spiritual complex, but modern science viewed him as a natural object set in a purely natural order of things. The old conceptions withdrew from the everyday world and lived on full of things that meant nothing to the souls of the workers.

The leading classes did not look for new substance for their consciousness, because they were able to hold on to the old that had been handed down to them. But the modern worker was torn out of his old setting. His life had been put on a totally new basis. For him there disappeared all possibility of drawing from the old spiritual springs.

Therefore the faith of the modern worker turned to the modern scientific conception of the world. Here he sought the new content that he needed for his inner consciousness. For the ruling classes the concept of a natural order of things leading up from the lowest animals to man remained purely theoretical, without an emotional content.

The worker took the scientific outlook in earnest and from it drew his own practical conclusions for life. It was the only thing left to him that had the power to awaken faith. Some may smile at this, but it is a fact of modern life on which the fate of the future turns. The educated man has made a pigeonhole for science in the recesses of his soul, but it is the circumstances of actual life that give the direction to his feelings.

The worker may be far from what others call scientific, yet his life's course is charted by such scientific lines of conception. For him science is turned into a creed of life, even though it be science filtered down to its last shallows and driblets of thought.

Now what scientific thought has not brought down from the old order is the consciousness of being rooted, as a spiritual type, in a spiritual world. For a member of the leading classes this presented no difficulty. Life, to him, was filled by the old traditions. But it was different for the worker. His new situation drove the old traditions from his soul. He took over from the leading classes a scientific mode of thought—a spiritual life that denied its spiritual origin.

I know very well how these thoughts will affect a lot of people. Believing they have a practical acquaintance with life, they look at the view expressed here as something remote from realities. But the language of actual facts, as voiced by the state of the world, will increasingly prove such a view as theirs to be a delusion.

I know, too, how someone professing working-class views will react to what has been said. I can hear him saying, "Just like the rest of them. Trying to shunt the real gist of the social question off onto lines that promise to be smooth for the bourgeois." He is unable to see that he himself lives as a working man but thinks as a bourgeois, using a type of thought inherited from them.

The scientific mode of conception will only become life-sustaining when, in its own fashion, it evolves an inner content. In its transition to the new age, the old spiritual life has turned into something which, for the working class, is ideology. The worker feels that this inner life does not come to him from a spiritual world of its own.

An important factor in the modern labor movement is this belief that spiritual life is ideology. It affects the worker's mood of soul as expressed in current social demands. Anyone who says that this idea exists only in the minds of the workers' leaders does not know what has been going on. The influence of this concept ties in with the demands of the Socialist and extends even to the deeds of those who "hatch revolution" out of the blind promptings of their inner life.

The non-worker listens with dismay to the worker saying, "Nothing short of socializing the means of production will make it possible for me to have a life worthy of a human being." But the non-worker is unable to form the faintest notion of how his own class, in the period of transition, not only summoned the worker to labor at means of production that were not his, but even failed to give him anything to satisfy and sustain the soul in his labor.

Worker and non-worker may both insist that the soul does not come into the picture, but such insistence does not touch the essence of the social question nor reveal its true form. For if the working population had inherited from the leading classes a genuine spiritual substance they would have had a different consciousness within their souls and would have voiced their social demands in a different fashion.

The unhappiness of the workers over the ideological character of spiritual life, even though they are not definitely conscious of it, makes them suffer acutely. In its significance for the social question today, it far outweighs all demands for an improvement in external conditions, justifiable as some of these demands may be.

The modern proletarian movement has sprung out of thoughts. I did not come to this conclusion as a result of lengthy pondering, but from years of actual experience and observation, when I was a lecturer at a workers' institute, giving instruction in a wide variety of subjects. And I have had occasion to go further and follow up the tendencies at work in the various unions and different occupational groups.

It is hard for members of the middle class today to put themselves into the soul of the worker or understand how the worker's still fresh, unexhausted intelligence opened up to receive a work such as that of Karl Marx. I am not proposing to discuss the substance of the Marxian system. This is not the significant thing. What seems to me significant above all else is the fact that the most powerful impulse at work in the labor world today is a thought system.

No practical movement, making the most matter-of-fact demands, has ever rested almost entirely on a basis of thought alone. Indeed it is in a way the first movement of its kind based completely on a scientific approach. But this must be seen in its proper light. Of main importance is the fact that thoughts have become the determining factor of the worker's attitude toward life while in other classes thoughts affect only the activity in the intellectual sphere.

Thus, what has become an inward reality in the worker is a reality that he cannot acknowledge because thought life has been handed down to him as an ideology. He really builds up his life upon thoughts, yet he feels thoughts to be unreal ideology. This inner contradiction, with all that it involves, must be clearly recognized. Otherwise, it is impossible to understand the workers' views of life and the way those who hold these views set about realizing them in practice.

One cannot expect a spiritual life that one feels as mere ideology to provide deliverance from a social situation one has resolved to endure no longer. The scientific cast of the modern worker's thought has turned not only science but also religion, art, morality and legal rights into so many constituent parts of human ideology. He fails to see behind these branches of the spiritual life the workings of an actual reality that exists in his own life and could contribute something to material existence. To him the intellectual sphere is only the mirror image of the material life. He is convinced that anything that will lead to the removal of social difficulties can arise only out of the sphere of the material processes themselves.

In fact the impotence of the spiritual life is an article of faith with a large part of the working class, and is openly stressed in Marxism and similar creeds. Yet the man obliged to lead the life of a worker today needs a spiritual life from which inner strength can come, strength to give him the sense of his own human dignity. The discovery of a path out of the maze of confusion into which social affairs have fallen depends on a right insight into this fact. The path has been blocked by the social system that has arisen, under the influence of the leading classes, with the new form of industrial economy. The strength to open it must be achieved.

In a human community where spiritual life plays a merely ideological role, the general social life lacks one of the forces that can make and keep it a living organism. The impotence of the spiritual life in modern man is what is ailing the body social today, and the disease is made worse by the reluctance to acknowledge its existence. Once this fact is acknowledged, there will be a basis on which to develop the kind of thinking needed for the social movement.

At present the worker thinks he has come in contact with a major force in his soul when he talks about his "class consciousness." The truth is that ever since he was caught up into the capitalistic economic machine he has been searching for a spiritual life that would sustain his soul and give him a consciousness of his human dignity. Yet there is no possibility of this with a spiritual life which he feels to be an ideology.

This human consciousness was what he was seeking. He could not find it, so he replaced it with "class consciousness" born of the economic life. His eyes are riveted on the economic life alone, as though some overpowering influence held them there. He no longer believes that anywhere in the spirit or in the soul can there be a latent force capable of supplying the impulse needed for the social movement. All he has faith in is that the evolution of the economic life, devoid of spirit and soul, can bring about the state of things he feels to be worthy of man. So he is driven to seek his welfare in a transformation of the economic life alone.

He has been forced to the conviction that with this mere transformation of the economic, all the social ills would disappear. He feels these ills were brought on through private enterprise, through the egoism of the individual employer, and also through the individual employer's powerlessness to do justice to the employee's claims of human self-respect. So he was led to believe that the only welfare for the body social lay in converting all private ownership of the means of production into a communal concern or into actual communal property. This conviction is due to people's eyes having, as it were, been removed from everything belonging to soul and spirit and fixed exclusively on the purely economic process.

Hence the paradox in the working-class movement. The modern worker believes that the economic life itself will, of necessity, develop everything that will ultimately give him his rights as man, the rights for which he is fighting. Yet in the heart of the fight something different makes its appearance, something which never could be an outcome of the economic life alone.

The fact is that this element lies in the direct line of evolution, through the old slave system, through the serfdom of the feudal age, to the modern proletariat of labor. This is what provides the fundamental force actuating the social purpose of the modern worker. It is related to the fact that the modern capitalistic system of economy recognizes basically nothing but commodities. In its processes something has been turned into a commodity which the worker feels must not and cannot be a commodity: the labor of the worker. If only the loathing that he feels at this were recognized as the fundamental force that it is!

Once people become aware of what this loathing means, they will have discovered the second of the two impulses making the current social question so urgent. The first, as was indicated earlier, is that spiritual life is felt as an ideology.

The fact that labor is still stamped with the character of a commodity has not remained unnoticed, but in studying it, people keep their attention fixed entirely on economic life. They see how the economic life gave the commodity character to human labor. What they do not see is that it is a necessity inherent in economic life that everything incorporated in it becomes a commodity.

Economic life consists in the production and useful consumption of commodities. One cannot divest human labor of its commodity character unless one finds a way of separating it from the economic process and bringing it under social forces that will do away with its commodity character. Any other form of industrial economy will only make labor a commodity in some other manner.

The labor question cannot take its place in its true form within the social question until it is recognized that the considerations of economic life (which determine the laws governing the circulation, exchange and consumption of commodities) are not considerations which should govern human labor.

Modern thinking has not learned to distinguish the totally different fashions in which the two things enter into economic life. On the one hand there is labor, which is intimately bound up with the human being himself. On the other hand there are those things that proceed from another source and are dissociated from the human being. The latter circulate along the paths that all commodities must take from their production to consumption. Sound thinking along these lines can show both the true form of the labor question as well as the proper place of economic life in a healthy society.

Thus we see that the "social question" divides itself into three distinct parts. The first is the question of a healthy form of spiritual life within the body social. The second is the consideration of labor, and the right way to incorporate it into the life of the community. Third is the correct deduction as to the proper place and function of economic life in today's society.

CHAPTER II

MEETING SOCIAL NEEDS

Our technically-based industrial economy, together with modern capitalism, has dictated the form in which the social problem presents itself today. Acting like a force of nature, it has given our social life its peculiar internal structure and ways of working. While men's attention was absorbed by what technical industry and capitalism brought with them, it became diverted from other spheres of the social life. Yet these also need direction by conscious human intelligence if the body social is to be healthy.

I may, perhaps, be allowed at this point to draw a comparison that will help in picturing what health in the body social implies. But keep in mind that this is a comparison only.

The human organism, that most complex of all natural organisms, can be described as consisting of three systems, working side by side. To a certain extent each functions separately and independently of the others. One of these consists of the life of the nerves and senses. It may be named, after the part where it is more or less centered, the head organism. Second, comes what we need to recognize as another branch if we really want to understand the human organism, the rhythmic system. This includes the breathing and the circulation of the blood, everything that finds expression in rhythmic processes in the human organism. The third must be recognized as consisting of all those organs that have to do with the actual transformation of matter—the metabolic process. These three systems comprise everything that, duly coordinated, keeps the whole human complex in healthy working order.

I have already attempted to give a brief description of this three-fold character of the natural human organism in my book, *Riddles of the Soul*. The approach tallies with what scientific research is on its way to telling us on this subject. It seems clear that biology, physiology and natural science in general, as it deals with man, are rapidly tending to a point of view that will show that what keeps the complex human organism in working order is just this comparatively separate functioning of its three separate systems. It follows that there is no such thing as absolute centralization in the human organism. Besides, each of these systems has its own special and distinct relation to the outer world; the head system through the senses, the rhythmic or circulatory system through the breathing, the metabolic system through the organs of nourishment and the organs of movement.

People may say that science can afford to wait until views such as these gain recognition all in good time, but the body social cannot afford to wait, either for right views or right practices. An understanding, even if only an instinctive one, of what the body social needs, is essential here. It cannot just be confined to a handful of experts, since every human soul has a share in the working of the body social. Sane thinking, feeling and willing as to the form to be given it can only be developed when one recognizes the fact that to thrive, the social organism, like the natural one, needs to be three-fold.

There have been many attempts lately to trace analogies between the organic structure of natural creatures and the structure of human society. What is said here has no connection with such approaches. Its object is simply to train human thought and feeling—using the human body as an object lesson—to a sense of what organic life requires. Such a perceptive sense can then be applied to the body social, which has its own laws.

The present crisis in human history demands the development of certain faculties of perception in every single human being. The first rudiments of these must be started by the schools and educational systems. The unconscious force in the soul that gave the body social its forms in the past will from now on cease to be active. Every individual is going to need to have these above-mentioned faculties of social perception. From now on the individual must be trained to have a healthy sense of how the forces of the body social have to work in order for it to live.

One hears much talk today about "socialization" as the thing that this age needs. This socialization, however, will prove to be no true cure, but rather, a quack remedy and possibly even a fatal one, unless there dawns in men's hearts and souls at least an instinctive perception of the necessity for the three-folding of the body social. If it is to function in a healthy way it must develop three organic members.

One of these three members is the *economic life.* It is the best one for us to begin considering here, because it has, through modern industry and modern capitalism, worked its way into the whole structure of human society to the subordination of everything else.

This economic life needs to form an independent, organic branch by itself within the body social. It must be relatively as independent as the nerves-and-senses system is within the human body. It is concerned with everything in the nature of the production of commodities, circulation of commodities and consumption of commodities.

Next comes the life of *public rights* (das Leben des öffentlichen Rechtes)—political life in the proper sense. This must be recognized as forming a second branch of the body social. To this branch belongs what one might term the true life of the state—taking Rights State in the sense in which the word was formerly applied to a community possessing common rights.

Economic life is concerned with all that a man needs from nature, and what he himself produces from nature, i.e., commodities, and their circulation and consumption. The second branch of the body social can have no other concern than with what is involved in purely human relations. It deals with what comes up from the deep recesses of the inner life and affects man's relations towards man. It is essential that one should clearly recognize the difference between the system of public rights and the economic system. The former can only deal, on an inner and purely human basis, with man-to-man relations. The economic system is concerned solely with the production, circulation and consumption of commodities. People must acquire an instinctive sense that enables them to distinguish between these two in life. This is essential so that in practice they will be kept as distinct as the work of the lungs is distinct, in the body, from what goes on in the nerves and sensory life.

The third division, alongside of the other two and equally independent, includes all those things in the social organism that are connected with the mental and spiritual life. The term, "spiritual culture," or, "everything that is connected with mental and spiritual life," hardly describes it accurately. Perhaps one might express it better as, "everything that rests on the natural endowments, both spiritual and physical, of each single human being."

The first system, the economic one, has to do with everything that must exist in order that man may regulate his material relationships to the world around him. The second, with whatever must exist in the body social because of the relationship of man to man. The third relates to all that springs from the personal individuality of each human being and that must be incorporated, from out of the personal individuality, in the body social.

Just as it is true that our social life has taken its imprint from modern industry and capitalism, so is it equally necessary that the injury thus unavoidably done to the body social should be healed. This can be done by bringing man, and the life of men with one another, into a correct relation to these three members of social life.

Economic life has recently, simply of its own accord, taken on quite new forms. Through one-sided activity it has asserted undue power and weight in human life. Meanwhile the other two branches have, up to now, not been in a position to work themselves into the social organism in a similarly matter-of-course way and to become incorporated with it according to their own proper laws. For them it is necessary that man step in, with the perception of which I have spoken, and set to work to evolve the social order. To attempt to solve the social problem in the way meant here will leave not one single individual without his task (working at the spot where he happens to be).

The first division of the body social, the economic life, is based primarily on conditions of nature. It is the same as with the individual man, the extent and scope of whose education and development rest on his individual qualities of mind and body. This nature-basis puts a unique stamp on economic life and, through it, on the whole social order. This nature-basis is inescapably there, and no methods of social organization, no manner of socializing measures can affect it. One must accept it as the groundwork of life for the body social. Every attempt at giving men's life in groups an economic form, must take it into account.

This is most obvious in extreme cases. Take for instance those parts of the earth where the banana affords man an easily accessible form of food. Here the question will be one of the amount and kind of labor to be expended to bring the banana from its place of origin to a convenient spot and deliver it ready for consumption. This will enter all considerations of men's life together. If one compares the human labor that must be exerted to make the banana ready for human consumption with that, for instance, which must be exerted in Central Europe to get wheat ready for consumption, the former is at least three hundred times less.

Of course that is an extreme case, but similar differences as to the necessary amounts of labor in relation to the nature-basis exist in the other branches of production represented in the various social communities of Europe. While they are not so marked, still they exist. So it is a basic factor in the body economic that the amount of labor-power that man has to put into the economic process is proportionate to the nature-basis on which he has to work. Take just for example the wheat yields in various countries of the world: in Germany, in districts of average fertility, the returns on wheat represent about a sevenfold to eightfold crop on the seed sown, in Chile it is twelvefold, in Northern Mexico seventeenfold, in Peru, twentyfold. (Jentsch, *Volkswirtschaftslehre,* p. 64).

The whole of this living complex of processes that begin with man's relation to nature and continue down to the point where nature's products are ready for consumption—these processes and these alone comprise, for a healthy social organism, its economic system. It occupies there somewhat the same place as that taken in the human organism by the head-system, which conditions the individual's abilities. But the head-system is dependent on the lung-and-heart system, and in the same way the economic system is dependent on the services of human labor. The head, however, cannot by itself regulate the breathing, and neither should the system of human labor-power be regulated by the forces that operate within the economic life itself.

It is through his interests that man is engaged in economic life, and the foundation of these is in the needs of his soul and spirit. In what way can a social organism most satisfactorily incorporate men's interests so that on the one hand the individual man finds in this social organism the best possible means of satisfying his personal interests, while at the same time he is economically employed to the best advantage? This is the question that has to be solved in a practical way in the institutions of the body economic. It can only be solved if these individual interests of men are given really free scope, and if at the same time there exist the will and the possibility of doing what is necessary to satisfy them.

These interests arise in a region outside the limits of the economic system. They develop as man's own inner and physical being unfolds. It is the business of economic life to make arrangements for their satisfaction. These arrangements, however, can only be concerned with the production and exchange of commodities—of goods which acquire their value from men's wants. The value of a commodity comes from the person consuming it. Because its value comes from the consumer, a commodity fills quite a different position in the social organism from other things that have a value for man as part of that organism. If one studies—without preconceptions—the whole circle of economic life, the production, circulation and consumption of commodities, one will see at once the difference in essential character between the relation that arises when one man makes commodities for another, and the human relation that must have its foundation on a rights relationship.

One will not stop with merely observing this difference. One will follow it up in a practical way and insist that economic life and the life of rights should be kept completely separate within the body social. Institutions for the production and exchange of commodities make men develop forms of activity not immediately productive of the best impulses for their mutual relations in rights. Man turns to his fellow man in the economic sphere because it suits their reciprocal interests. Radically different is the link between man and man in the rights life.

One might perhaps think that the distinction between the two branches is adequately recognized if the institutions of the economic life also make provisions for the rights involved in the mutual relations of the people engaged in it, but such an idea has no root in reality. The relation in rights that necessarily exists between a man and his fellows can only be felt and lived outside the economic sphere, on totally different soil, not inside it. So there must be, in the healthy social organism, another system of life alongside and independent of the economic life, where human rights can develop and find suitable administration.

The rights life is, strictly speaking, the political sphere, the true sphere of the state. If the interests men have to serve in their economic life are carried over into the legislation and administration of the rights state, then these rights will merely be an expression of economic interests. At the same time, if the rights state takes on the management of economic affairs, it is no longer fitted to rule men's life of rights. All that it does and establishes will be forced to serve man's need for commodities, and as a result, be diverted from those impulses that make for the life of rights.

That is why a healthy social organism requires the independent political life of the state as a second branch alongside the economic sphere. In the economic complex, men will be guided by the forces of economic life itself in the production and interchange of commodities. In the state, institutions will arise where dealings between individuals and groups will be settled on lines that satisfy men's sense of right.

This demand for a complete separation of the rights state from the economic sphere is based on life as it actually is. Those who seek to combine the two are not proceeding realistically. Of course people engaged in economic life possess the sense of right, but they will only be able to legislate and administrate from a sense of right alone (without mixing economic interests in) when they come to consider questions of right independently in a rights state. Such a state takes no part in economic life.

This rights state, with its legislature and administration, will be built up on those human impulses which nowadays go by the name "democratic." The legislative and administrative bodies in the economic domain will arise out of the forces of economic life. Transactions between the executive heads of the two spheres will be carried on much as those between governments of sovereign states are handled today. They will influence each other in a healthy way that is impossible when their functions are intermingled.

So just as, on the one hand, the economic life is subjected to the conditions of the nature-basis, it is, on the other hand, dependent on those relations in right that the state establishes between individuals and groups engaged in economic work. In this way the boundaries are designated for the proper and possible activities of economic life.

In the present social organism as developed in the course of historical evolution, economic life occupies an unduly large place. It sets upon the whole social movement the peculiar stamp it has acquired from the machine age and modern capitalism. It has come to include more than it should include in any healthy society. In present-day economic trading, where only commodities should be dealt in, we find also human labor and human rights. At present one can trade, within the economic sphere that rests on the division of labor, not only commodities for commodities but commodities for human labor—and for human rights as well.

By "commodity" I mean everything that, through human activity, has acquired the form in which it is finally brought by man to its place of destination for consumption. Economists may perhaps find this definition objectionable or inadequate, but it may be serviceable towards an understanding of what properly belongs to economic life.*

When anyone acquires a plot of land by purchase, one must regard it as an exchange of the land for commodities for which the purchase money stands as the proxy. The plot of land, however, does not act as a commodity in the economic life. It holds its position in the body social through the right the owner has to use it. There is an essential difference between this right-of-use and the relation of a producer to the commodity he produces.

---

* *Author's Note:* For the purposes of life, what is wanted in an explanation is not definitions drawn from theory but ideas that give a picture of a real, live process. As used in this sense, "commodity" denotes something that plays an actual part in man's life and experience. Any other concept of it either omits or adds to this and so fails to tally exactly with what really and truly goes on in life.

From the very nature of the producer's relation to his product, it cannot enter the totally different, man-to-man relation created by somebody's having been granted the sole right to use a certain piece of land. Other men are obliged to live on this land, or the owner sets them to work on it for their living. Thus he brings them into a state of dependence upon himself. On the other hand, the fact of mutually exchanging genuine commodities that one produces or consumes, does not establish a dependence that affects the man-to-man relation in the same kind of way.

To an unprejudiced mind it is clear that a fact of actual life such as this, must, in a healthy society, find due expression in its social institutions. So long as there is simply an interchange of commodities for commodities in economic life, the value of these is determined independently of relations-of-right. As soon as commodities are interchanged for rights, the rights relation is itself affected.

The exchange in itself is not the question here. Such an exchange is inevitable in the modern social organism, which rests on division of labor. The point is that through this interchange of rights and commodities rights themselves are turned into a commodity when the source of right lies within the economic life. The only way of preventing this is by having two sets of institutions in the body social. The sole object of the one is to conduct commodities most efficiently along its circuit. The other regulates those rights involved in commodity exchange—rights that arise between individuals engaged in producing, trading and consuming. These are not distinct in their nature from any other rights, because they deal with the relationship from man to man. They fall in the same category as any other injury or benefit caused by some action or negligence in which the exchange of commodities is not involved.

In the life of the individual the effects of the rights establishment merge with those of purely economic activity. In the healthy social organism they must come from two different directions. What matters in the economic sphere is the proper education and training of the leading personalities, as well as their competence and experience. In the rights organization laws and administration will give expression to the general sense of what is right in men's dealings with each other.

The economic organization will assist the formation of Associations among people who, from their occupation or as consumers, have the same interests or similar requirements. This network of Associations, working together, will build up the whole fabric of the industrial economy. The economic organization will grow up on an associative basis and out of the links between the Associations. Their work will be purely economic in character, and will be carried out on the basis of rights provided by the rights organization.

These Associations, being able to get their economic interests recognized in the representative and administrative bodies of the economic organization, will not feel any need to force themselves into the legislature or the executive branch of the rights state—as for instance a Landowners' League, a Manufacturers' Party or an economically oriented Socialist Party. They will not try to effect in the rights state what they have no power to achieve within the limits of the economic life.

Then again, if the rights state takes no part whatever in any branch of industrial economy, the institutions it establishes will only be such as spring from a sense of right among its members. Although those sitting in its representative body may, and of course will, be the same people who are taking an active part in economic life, nevertheless, owing to the division of the economic and rights life, the health of the body social will not be undermined. Economic life will not be able to exert such an influence on the rights life as can happen when the state itself organizes branches of economic life. In that case, representatives of the economic world sit as political legislators, making laws to suit economic interests.

A person in public life today usually turns his attention to secondary considerations. This is because his habits of thought lead him to regard the body social as uniform in structure. As such, however, there is no form of suffrage he can devise that will fit it. The economic interests and the impulses of human rights will come into conflict in the legislature, no matter how it is elected. This conflict will affect social life in a way that is bound to bring severe shocks to the whole organism of society.

The first and indispensable thing to be worked for in public life today must be the complete and thorough separation of economic life from the rights organization. As the separation becomes gradually established and people grow into it, something else will happen. The two organizations will, in the course of this process, each discover its own most appropriate method of selecting its legislators and administration.

Where the old conditions still exist, these can be taken as the basis from which to work towards the new separation of functions. Where the old order has already melted away or is in process of dissolution, individuals and small groups of people must find the initiative to start reconstructing along the new lines of growth. To try in twenty-four hours to bring about a transformation in public life is recognized by thoughtful socialists themselves as midsummer madness. They look to gradual, opportune changes to bring about what they regard as social welfare. The light of facts, however, must make it plain to any impartial observer that a reasoning will and purpose are needed to make a new social order. These are imperatively demanded by the forces at work in mankind's historical evolution.

Those who regard such remarks as "impractical" are the very people whose way of thinking helped to bring about the present state of affairs.

There must be a reversal of the movement in leading circles that has already brought various departments of economic life—the postal and railway services, etc.—into state ownership. There must be a movement towards eliminating all economic activity from the domain of politics and state organization. Thinkers whose aim, as they believe, is the welfare of society, take the movement towards state control that was started by the previously governing circles, and push it to its logical extreme. They propose to socialize all institutions of economic life insofar as they are means of production.

A healthy course of development, however, will give economic life its independence. At the same time it will give the political state a system of right through which it can bring its influence to bear on the body economic. This influence will be such that the individual shall not feel that his function within the body social violates his sense of right.

When one considers the work that a man does for the body social by means of his physical labor, it is plain that the above remarks are grounded in the actual life of men. The position that labor has come to occupy in the social order under the capitalistic form of economy is such that it is purchased by the employer (from the employed) as a commodity. An exchange is effected between money (as representing commodities) and labor. In reality no such exchange can take place. It only appears to do so.* What really

---

* *Author's note.* It is quite possible in life for a transaction not only to be interpreted un-

happens is that the employer receives in return from the worker commodities that cannot exist unless the latter devotes his labor-power to creating them. The worker receives one part, the employer the other part of the value of the commodity so created. The production of the commodity is the result of a cooperation between employer and employed. The product of their joint action is what first passes into the circuit of economic life.

For the product to come into existence there must be a relation in rights between worker and enterpriser. But the capitalist type of economy is able to convert this rights relation into one determined by the employer's superiority in economic power over the employed. In a healthy social order it will be obvious that labor cannot be paid for, for one cannot set an economic value upon it comparable to the value of a commodity. The commodity produced by this labor first acquires an economic value by comparison with other commodities. The kind of work a man must do for the maintenance of the body social, how he does it, and the amount, must be settled according to his abilities and the conditions of a decent human existence. This is only possible when such questions are settled by the political state, quite independently of the provisions and regulations made in the economic life.

This definition of labor as being independent of the economic life establishes a new basis of values comparable to the one already established by the conditions of nature. The value of one commodity as measured by another is increased by the fact that its raw material is more difficult to procure. Similarly the value of a commodity

realistically but also to take place unrealistically. Money and labor are not interchangeable values, but only money and the products of labor. Accordingly, if I give money for labor, I am doing something that is unreal. I am making a sham transaction, for in reality I can only give money for the product of labor.

must be made dependent on the kind and amount of labor that the rights system allows to be expended on its production.*

So the economic life has its conditions fixed on two sides. There is the nature-basis, which man must take as he finds it. On the other side there will be the rights-basis, which should be created on the free and independent ground of the political state. This activity will be detached from economic life and come up out of the common sense of right.

It is obvious that in such a social organism the standard of living (economic well-being) will rise and fall with the amount of labor that the sense of right, felt by all in common, expends on it, but this must be so in a healthy society. The subordination of the general economic prosperity to the common sense of right is the only thing that can prevent man from being so used up and consumed by economic life that his existence no longer seems to him worthy of a human being. It is this sense of an existence unworthy of human beings that is really at the bottom of social convulsions.

If the general standard of economic well-being should become too much lowered on the rights side, there is a way of preventing this. It is the same as with the nature-basis, where technical means can be used to make a less productive soil more productive. So, if prosperity declines too much, the methods and amount of work can be changed. Only it should be realized that such changes must not be a direct consequence of processes in the economic life. They should be the outcome of insight arrived at on the free ground of rights, independent of economic life.

* *Author's Note.* This relationship of labor to the rights system will have to be accepted by the Associations as a given premise in economic life. What this does, however, is to make the economic system dependent on man instead of man being dependent on the system of economics.

There is, however, still another element that enters into everything contributed towards the organization of social life, whether by the economic side or the rights-consciousness. This comes from a third source, the personal abilities of the individual. It includes everything from the loftiest achievements of the mind to the products of bodily activity. A healthy social organism must necessarily take up and assimilate what it gets from this source differently than what comes to it from the life of the state or all that is expressed in the interchange of commodities.

The only healthy way this element can be absorbed into social life is by depending upon the receptivity of people, and on the impulses that go with personal ability. If the deeds resulting from such human faculties are subjected to the artificial influence of the economic sphere and rights system they will lose their true foundation. The foundation for this kind of activity lies in that force in man that develops through the human performance itself. A free, spontaneous receptivity on the part of the public is the only sound and wholesome channel for the reception of such creative work. If its acceptance depends on the economic life or on the state, there is a check on such independent public reaction.

There is only one possible line of healthy evolution for the spiritual-cultural life of the body social. What it does must come out of its own impulses, and those served by it must be connected with it by close ties of sympathy and understanding. Parenthetically, we must point out the need of remembering by what countless, fine threads this spiritual life is connected with the evolution of all other human potentialities.

Here we have sketched the necessary conditions for a sound evolution of the spiritual life of the body social. People do not see this clearly because they are used to seeing the spiritual life fused and confused with the state system. This fusing process has been going on for several hundred years and people have become used to it. They talk about "freedom of knowledge" and "freedom of education," but consider it a matter of course that the political state should have control of this "free" knowledge and "free" education. They neither see nor feel how, in this way, the state is bringing all spiritual life into a dependence on state requirements.

The notion is that the state provides the educational posts and the spiritual life then unfolds "freely" under the hands of the people who fill these state posts. People come to forget the intimate connection between the innermost nature of man and the content of the spiritual life growing up within him. They do not realize that it is impossible for the growth of this spiritual content to be really free if it owes its place in the body social to any other impulses than those that proceed from the spiritual life itself.

Science has received its whole mold and form from its being under state management in recent centuries, and with it all that part of the spiritual life that it affects. This fusion with the state has affected its content, its inner substance, as well. Of course, the results of mathematics or physics cannot be directly influenced by the state, but have not history and other subjects of general culture come to be an obedient mirror of state requirements?

The peculiar stamp that our mental conceptions, which are predominantly scientific, have acquired in this way is just what makes them a mere ideology as far as the workers are concerned. They see how the character of men's thoughts rises out of the requirements of a state life that suits the interests of the ruling classes. They saw a reflection of interests and the war of interests. So they developed a feeling that all spiritual life was ideology, a mirror image of the economic order.

Such a view works havoc with men's spiritual life, but the blight will cease when men can feel that in the spiritual sphere there rules a reality of its own. It is one that transcends outer material life and carries its own inner substance in itself. No such sense of a spiritual reality can possibly arise, however, unless the spiritual life is free within the body social to expand and govern* itself according to its own impulses.

An independent position in society is an absolute necessity for art, science and a philosophy of life—along with all that goes with them. For in spiritual life everything is interrelated. State requirements cannot directly influence the substance of mathematics, for instance, or physics, but state requirements do influence the way such things are applied and the estimation put on them, whenever some branches of spiritual life are under state control.

It is quite a different thing when the teacher in the lowest grade in school follows the state line than when he takes his line from a spiritual life that rests on its own, independent footing. Here again the Social Democrats have simply taken over a habit of thought from the ruling classes when they have the ideal of incorporating the spiritual life into a social structure based on a system of industrial economy. If they accomplished this it would simply be a fur-

---

* *Translator's Note:* References in this book to the *governing* of the spiritual-cultural sphere, or to the spiritual-cultural *organization* are most definitely not to be understood as anything like the "government" or "organizing" of personal cultural activity, as a present-day reader might think. The author's concept of an organization of this branch of the body social simply means a group of representatives of the free institutions of the spiritual sphere, such as universities, schools, museums, religious bodies, etc. etc., with delegated authority to handle problems arising in this sphere and to deal with the other two branches of the Threefold Social Order.

ther step along the road that has led to the present depreciation of spiritual life.

The socialist maxim, "Religion is a man's private affair," expressed what is a right perception, but in a one-sided way. In a healthy society all spiritual life must in this sense be a private affair as far as the state and economic life are concerned. But their idea was not to give religion a better chance to develop, rather that religion should not be fostered by the body social because it is not anything it needs.

When teachers, artists and others have no direct connection with any legislature or government they will find they have an altogether different influence. They will be able to awaken an understanding for what they are creating. Also, things will be different when they are appealing to people who are not simply under compulsion to labor, but for whom an independent, autonomous political state also insures the right to leisure. Leisure awakens the mind to an appreciation of spiritual values.

At this point somebody will probably tell you, out of "practical experience," that if the state made definite provision for people to have leisure hours, and at the same time school attendance were left to their own common sense, they would simply spend all their leisure in bars and taverns and would relapse into illiteracy. Let such pessimists wait and see what will happen when the world is no longer under their influence. Too often, their approach is inspired by a feeling of how they themselves like to spend their leisure hours, and memory of what they had to do to get a little "education." Naturally, they take no account of the free spiritual life and its power to enkindle. They only know the spiritual life in bondage, and it has no power to light any sparks in them.

When the body-spiritual of society is administering itself, both

34

the state and the economic system will get from it that steady inflow from the spiritual life of which they are in need. Also, when the economic and spiritual bodies can cooperate in freedom it will be found that practical training for the economic life will, for the first time, be able to develop its full possibilities. People will come, suitably trained, into the economic field, and put life into everything they meet there, with the strength they derive from the liberated treasures of the spiritual, and people with economic experience will find their way into the spiritual organization and help fructify what needs fructifying there.

Within the political state, the effect of spiritual abilities being left free, will be the growth of sane and sound views—which are needed in this field. As a result of such abilities, the man who works with his hands will find a place in the body social that will give him satisfaction. He will get a sense of the inter-connection of his own labor with those organizing forces that he can trace to the development of individual human talents. The political state will give him a basis on which he can establish the rights that secure to him his share of the returns from the commodities he produces. He will also freely allot to the spiritual property, from which he benefits, a sufficient portion to keep it productive.

There will be a possibility for producers in the spiritual-cultural field to live on the proceeds of their work. What anyone chooses to do in the matter of such work will be nobody's affair but his own. For any service he may render to the body social, he will be able to count on willing recompense from people to whom spiritual goods are a necessity. Anyone who cannot find what he requires through the recompense he gets under the spiritual organization, will have to go over to one of the other fields, either the political state or the economic life.

Into the economic life there flow the technical ideas which originate in the spiritual life. Their origin is in that realm even though they come directly from people belonging to the state sphere or to the economic world. For all those ideas and organizing capacities that enrich the life of the state and of industrial economy originate in the spiritual life. The recompense for everything supplied to these fields from the spiritual will either be raised voluntarily by the beneficiaries, or else be regulated by the rights that are developed in the political sphere.

What the political state itself needs for its own maintenance will be raised by a system of taxation. This will be the outcome of a harmonious coordination of the claims of economic life and of the rights-consciousness.

It must be reiterated that in a healthy society there must, alongside the political and the economic, be the spiritual sphere functioning independently on its own footing. The whole trend of the evolutionary force of modern mankind is in the direction of this threefolding of the social organism. As long as the social life could be guided in all its essentials by the instinctive forces at work in the mass of mankind, there was no urgent tendency towards this definite membering into three functions. Basically, there were always these three, but in a still dim, and dully conscious, social life they worked together as one. Our modern age demands of man that he place himself consciously into the social organism. This new social consciousness, however, must be orientated from three sides if it is to shape men's life and conduct in a healthy way. It is this threefold line of evolution that modern humanity is striving towards in the soul's unconscious depths. What finds an outlet in the social movement is simply a dulled reflection of this striving.

At the end of the Eighteenth Century, under different circumstances from ours today, there went up a cry from the hidden depths of human nature for a re-formation of social relations. One could hear, like a motto of this reorganization, the three words, "Fraternity, Equality, Liberty." While normal human feelings for the realities cannot fail to sympathize with all that these three words imply, there were keen thinkers during the Nineteenth Century who took pains to point out the impossibility of realizing these three ideas in any homogeneous and uniform society. It seemed clear to them that they must contradict one another if actually carried into practice. For instance, it was cleverly demonstrated that if the impulse towards equality were realized there would be no possible room for the freedom that is inherent in every human being.

These three ideals appear contradictory until one perceives the necessity of establishing a threefold order of society. Then their real meaning for social life first becomes apparent. The three divisions must not be artificially dovetailed and centralized under some theoretical scheme of unity. They must be one living reality. Each of the three branches of the body social must center in itself. The unity of the whole social organism will first come about through the workings of the three, side by side and in combination. For in actual life it is the apparent contradictions that make up a unity.

One will come to comprehend what the life of the body social is when one perceives fully the part played by these three principles of brotherhood, equality and freedom in a real, workable form of society. Then it will be recognized that men's cooperation in economic life must rest on the brotherhood that springs up out of the Associations.

The second system is that of common rights, where one is dealing with purely human relations between one person and another. Here one must strive to realize the idea of equality.

In the spiritual field, which stands in comparative independence in the body social, it is the idea of freedom that needs to be realized.

Seen in this way, these three ideals reveal their value for real existence. They can find realization neither in a chaotic social life nor in a social state constructed on an abstract, centralized scheme, but only in the threefold working of a healthy social organism. There, each of the three branches can derive its strength from one of these ideal impulses, and all three branches will work fruitfully in conjunction.

Those people at the end of the Eighteenth Century who first demanded recognition of these three ideas, freedom, equality, brotherhood, already had a dim sense of where the forces of human evolution were tending. So also did those who took up the cry again later on. They still believed in the Onefold State, where these ideas involve a contradiction. They nevertheless pinned their faith to this contradiction because in their subconscious depths there was this striving towards the Threefold Order of Society, in which their triad can achieve a higher unity.

To lay hold of these evolutionary forces that are working towards the Threefold Order, and to make of them a conscious social will and purpose, is what is demanded of us at the present time. It is demanded in unmistakable language by the hard facts of the social situation.

CHAPTER III

CAPITALISM AND CREATIVE SOCIAL IDEAS
(Capital and Human Labor)

The only way to get a sound judgment as to what action is needed in the social field is through insight into the basic forces at work in the social organism. The basic idea behind the preceding chapters was an attempt to arrive at such an insight. The facts of social life show that the social disturbances are not merely on the surface but are fundamental. Vision that penetrates to the foundations is needed to cope with them.

It is in capital and capitalism that the worker looks for the cause of his grievances. But to arrive at any fruitful conclusion as to capital's part, for good or ill, in the social structure, one has first to be perfectly clear as to how capital is produced and consumed. One has to learn how this process takes place as a result of the individual abilities of people and the effects of the rights system and the forces of economic life.

One points to human labor as the factor that, together with capital and the nature-basis of the economy, creates the economic values. Through these three factors, the worker becomes conscious of

39

his social situation. To reach any conclusion as to the way in which human labor must be placed into the social organism without injuring the worker's self-respect, requires keeping in mind the relation of human labor to the development of individual abilities, and to the rights-consciousness.

Today, quite rightly, people are asking what the first step must be (the most immediate action) if the claims presented by the social movement are to be met. Even a first step will not succeed unless we first know how it is to be related to the basic principles of a healthy social order. Once this is known, then, in whatever part of the social structure one is working, one will discover the particular thing that requires doing. What keeps people from this insight is the fact that they take their opinions from the social institutions themselves. Their thoughts follow the lead of the facts instead of mastering them. Today, however, we need to see that no adequate judgment can be formed without going back to those primal creative thoughts that underlie all social institutions.

The body social requires a constant, fresh supply of the forces residing in these primal thoughts. If the suitable channels for these thoughts are not there, then social institutions take on forms that impede life instead of furthering it. Yet the primal thoughts live on in men's instinctive impulses, even if their conscious thoughts are mistaken and build up stumbling blocks. It is these primal thoughts that come to expression, openly or in a hidden way, in the revolutionary convulsions of the social order.

Such convulsions will only cease when the body social takes a form in which two things are possible: First, an inclination to notice when an institution is beginning to deviate from its original intention, and second, the counteracting of every such deviation before it becomes strong enough to be a danger.

In our times the actual conditions have come to deviate widely from the demand of the primal thoughts. We need to turn vigorously back to these primal thoughts and not dismiss them as "impractical" generalities. From them we need to learn the direction in which the actual realities must now be consciously guided, for the time has gone by in which the old, instinctive guidance sufficed for mankind.

One of the basic questions raised by the practical criticism of the times is how to put a stop to the oppression the worker suffers under private capitalism. The owner, or manager, of capital is in a position to put other men's bodily labor into the service of what he undertakes to produce.

It is necessary to distinguish three elements in the social relation that arises in the cooperation of capital and human labor-power. First, there is the enterprising activity, which must rest on the individual ability of some person or group of persons. Second, the relation of the entrepreneur to the worker, which must be a relation in right. Third is the production of an object, which acquires a commodity value in the circuit of economic life.

For the enterprising activity to come to expression in a healthy way, there must be forces at work in social life that let individual abilities function in the best possible way. This can only happen if the body social includes a sphere that gives an able person the freedom to use his capacities, and leaves the judgment of their value to the free and voluntary understanding of others.

It is clear that what a man can do socially by means of capital comes into the sphere of society where the laws and the administration are taken care of by the spiritual life. If the political state interferes to influence these personal activities, the decisions will unavoidably show a lack of understanding of individual abilities. This

41

is because the political state is necessarily based on what is similar and equal in all men's claims on life. It is its business to translate this equality into practice. Within its own domain it must make sure that every man has a fair chance to make his personal opinion count. Its proper work has nothing to do with understanding individual abilities, so it ought never to have any influence on the exercise of these.

Just as little, where capital is needed for something, should the prospect of economic advantage determine the exercise of individual abilities. Many, weighing the pros and cons of capitalism, put great stress on this prospect. In their opinion it is only this incentive that can induce individual ability to exert itself. As "practical men," they refer to the "imperfections of human nature." There is no doubt that in the social order under which the present state of things developed, the prospect of economic advantage has come to play a very important part. The fact is that to no small extent, this is the cause of the state of things today. Thus there is need for the development of some other, different incentive. This can only be found in the social sense that will develop out of a healthy spiritual life. Out of the strength of the free spiritual life, a man's education and schooling will send him into activity equipped with impulses that will lead him, thanks to this social sense, to making real the things toward which his individual capacities drive him.

Visionary illusions have certainly caused tremendous harm in social endeavor, as in other fields, but such a point of view as that expressed above need not come into the "visionary" category. What is stated here does not rest on any notion that "the spirit" will work wonders if only the people who think they are filled with it, continually speak about it. It comes, on the contrary, out of observation of how people actually do work when they work together freely in the spiritual field. This work in common takes on a social character of its own accord, provided only that it can develop in real freedom.

It is only the lack of freedom in spiritual life that has kept its social character from coming to expression. The spiritual forces of social life have come to expression among the leading classes in a way that has, anti-socially, restricted their use and value to limited circles. What was produced in these circles could only be brought to the workers in an artificial way. They could get from it no support for their souls, because they did not really have any part in it. Schemes for popular education, for "uplifting the masses" to appreciation of art, etc., are no way of spreading spiritual property among "the people," for "the people" are not within its life. All that can be given them is a view of these treasures from a point outside.

This also applies to those offshoots of spiritual activity that find their way into economic life on the basis of capital. In a healthy social order the worker should not merely stand at his machine while the capitalist alone knows what is going to become of the products in the circuit of economic life. The worker should be able to form a conception of the part he is playing in society through his work on the production line. Conferences, regarded as much a part of the operation as the work itself, should be held regularly by the management. Their aim will be the developing of a common set of ideas for the employed and the employer. Such activity will bring the workers to a sense of the fact that control of capital, properly carried out, benefits the whole community, including the worker. Also, an approach aimed at promoting a full understanding, will make the employer careful to keep his business methods above suspicion.

Only those unable to appreciate the effects of the community of feeling that arises from sharing a common task will consider the

43

foregoing to be meaningless. Others will see clearly the benefits to economic productivity that will come from having the direction of economic affairs rooted in the free spiritual life. If this preliminary condition is fulfilled the present interest in capital and its increase merely for the sake of profits, would be replaced by a practical interest in producing something and getting work done.

The socialistic-minded thinkers of today are struggling to get the means of production under the control of society. What is legitimate in their aims can only be achieved if this control is exercised by the free spiritual sphere of society. In that way economic compulsion, which goes out from the capitalist and which is felt as something unworthy of human beings, will be made impossible. Such compulsion arises when the capitalist acts out of the forces of economic life. At the same time the crippling of men's individual abilities, which results when these abilities are governed by the political state, will not arise.

Earnings on everything done through capital and individual ability must result, like the results of all other spiritual work, from the free initiative of the doer and the free appreciation of those who wish the work done. A man himself must estimate what these earnings must be, taking into consideration preliminary training, incidental expenses, etc. Whether he finds his claims gratified or not depends on the appreciation his services meet with.

Social arrangements on such lines will lay the basis for a really free contractual relationship between the employer (work-director) and the work-doer. It will rest, not on barter of commodities, or money, for labor, but on an agreement as to the share due to each of the two joint producers of the commodity.

The sort of service rendered to the body social on the basis of capital depends, from its very nature, on the way in which individual human capacities reach into the social organism. Nothing but the free spiritual life can give men's abilities the impulse they need for their development. Even in a society where this development is tied up with the political state administration or with the forces of economic life, real productivity in things requiring the expenditure of capital depends on the extent to which free individual capacities can force their way through the hindrances imposed on them. Under such conditions, however, the development is not a healthy one. This free development of individual ability, using capital as a basis, is not what has brought about the commodity status of human labor power, but, rather is it the shackling of labor-power by the political state or by the circuit of economic processes.

Recognition of this fact is a necessary preliminary to everything that has to be done by way of social organization. For the superstition has grown up that the measures needed (for the health of society) must come from either the state or the economy. If we go any farther along the road on which this superstition has led us, we shall be setting up all sorts of institutions that will make oppressive conditions increasingly worse instead of leading man towards the goal he is striving for.

People learned to think about capitalism at a time when it had induced a disease in the body social. They experience the disease, and see that something must be done about it, but they must see more, namely, that the disease originates in the absorption into the economic circuit of the forces at work in capital. If one wants to work in the direction called for by the forces of human evolution, one must not be deluded into considering as "impractical idealism" the idea that the management of capital should be in the sphere of the free spiritual life.

At present people are little inclined to connect the idea that is to lead capitalism in a healthy direction, with the free spiritual life. Rather they connect it with something in the circuit of the economic life. They see how production has led to large scale industry and this, in turn, to the present form of capitalism. Now they propose to replace this by a system of syndicates that will work to meet the wants of the producers themselves. Since, of course, industry must retain all the modern means of production, the various industrial concerns are to be united into one big syndicate. Here, they think, everyone will be producing to meet the orders of the community, and the community cannot be an exploiter because it would simply be exploiting itself. Since they must link onto something that already exists, they turn their attention to the modern state, with the idea of converting it into a comprehensive syndicate.

What they leave out of account is that the bigger the syndicate, the less likelihood of its being able to do what they expect of it. Unless individual ability finds its place in the organism of the syndicate, in the manner and the form already described, the community control of labor cannot lead to healing of the social organism.

People are unwilling to look without bias at the idea of the spiritual life taking an active part in the social organism because they are used to thinking of it as at the opposite pole from everything material and practical. Many will find something grotesque in the view presented here, namely, that a part of the spiritual life should manifest itself in the activity of capital in the economic life. It is conceivable that on this point members of what have been up to now the ruling classes, may find themselves in agreement with socialistic thinkers. To see what this supposed absurdity means for the health of the body social requires that we examine certain present-day currents of thought. These, springing from impulses in the soul, are quite honest in their fashion, but they check the development of any really social way of thinking wherever they find entrance.

These thought currents tend, more or less unconsciously, away from everything that gives energy and driving power to inner experience. They aim at a world conception, an inner life, that strives for scientific knowledge as an island in the general sea of existence. One finds people who think it "distinguished" to sit in cloud castles meditating abstractly on all sorts of ethical and religious problems, such things as virtue and how best to acquire it, how to find an "inner significance" for one's life, etc. One sees how impossible it is to build a bridge between what these people call good, and everything that is going on in the outer world. There, in men's everyday surroundings, we see what is happening with the manipulation of capital, the payment of labor, the consumption, production and circulation of commodities, the system of credit, of banking, and the stock exchange.

One can see two main streams running side by side even in people's very habits of thought. One of them remains aloft, as it were, in divine-spiritual heights, and has no desire to build a bridge from spiritual impulses to life's ordinary activities. The other stream runs on, void of thought, in the everyday world.

But life is a single whole. It cannot thrive unless the forces that dwell in all ethical and religious life bring driving power to the commonplace, everyday things of life—that life that some people may think a bit beneath them. For if people neglect building a bridge between the two regions of life, then not only their religious and moral life, but also their social thinking degenerates into mere wordy sentiment, far removed from everyday reality. This reality then has its revenge. Out of a sort of "spiritual" impulse man goes on striving after every imaginable ideal, and everything he calls "good," but to those instincts that underlie the ordinary daily needs of life (the ones that need an economic system for their satisfaction), he devotes himself minus his "spirit." He knows no pathway between the two realms, and so everyday life gets a form that is not even supposed to have any connection with those ethical impulses. Then the ordinary things of every day are avenged, for the ethical, religious life turns to a living lie in men's hearts because (without this being noticed) it is being separated from all direct contact with life.

How many people there are today who, out of a certain ethical or religious quality of mind, have the will to live on a right footing with their fellow men. They really want to deal with others only in the best way imaginable, but they cannot lay hold of any social conception that expresses itself in practical habits of life.

It is people like these who, at this epoch-making moment when social questions have become so urgent, are actually blocking the road to a true practice of life. They see themselves as practical while they are, in fact, visionary obstructionists. One can hear them making speeches like this:

"What is really needed is for people to rise above all this materialism, this external material life that drove us into the disaster of the great war and into all this misery. People must turn to a spiritual conception of life."

To illustrate man's path to spirituality, they harp on great men of the past who were venerated for their spiritual way of thinking. When one tries to bring the talk around to the thing the spirit has to do for practical life, the creation of daily bread, one is reminded that the first thing, after all, is to bring people again to acknowledge the spirit.

At this moment, however, the urgent thing is to employ the powers of the spiritual life to discover the right principles of social health. For this it is not enough that men make a hobby of the spirit. Everyday existence needs to be brought into line with the spirit. It was this taste for turning spiritual life into bypaths that led the classes that have been ruling up to now, to favor the social conditions that ended in the present state of affairs.

In contemporary society, the management of capital for the production of commodities, and the ownership of the means of production (thus also of capital) are tightly bound together. Yet the effects in the social system of these two relationships between man and capital—management and ownership—are quite different. The control, the management, of capital by individual ability is, when suitably applied, a means—to everybody's interest—of enriching the body social with goods. Whatever a person's position in life, it is to his interest that there should be no waste of those individual abilities that flow from the springs of human nature. Through them are created goods that are of use to the life of man. Yet these abilities are never developed unless the people endowed with them have free initiative in their exercise. Any check to the free flow from these sources means a certain measure of loss to human welfare, but capital is the means for making these abilities available for wide spheres of social life.

To administer the total amount of capital in such a way that specially gifted individuals or qualified groups can get the use of it to apply it as their particular initiative prompts them, must be to the true interests of everybody in a community. Everybody, brainworker or laborer, must say (if he steers clear of prejudice and consults his own interests):

"I not only wish an adequate number of persons, or groups of people, to have absolutely independent use of capital, but I should also like them to have access to it on their own initiative. For they themselves are the best judges of how their particular abilities can make capital a means of producing what is useful to the body social."

It does not fall within the scope of this work to describe how, as individual human abilities came to play a part in the social order, private property grew up out of other forms of ownership. Up to the present day this form of ownership has, under the influence of the division of labor, gone on developing within the body social. It is with present conditions, and the necessary next stage of their evolution, that we are concerned here.

In whatever way private property arose—by the exercise of power, conquest, etc.—it is an outcome of the social creativeness that is associated with individual human ability. Yet Socialists today, with their thoughts bent on social reconstruction, hold the theory that the only way to get rid of what is oppressive in private ownership is to turn to communal ownership. They put the question this way: How can private possession of the means of production be prevented, so that its oppressive effect on the unpropertied masses may cease? In putting the question this way, they overlook the fact that the social organism is something that is constantly developing, growing. About a growing organism one cannot ask: What is the best arrangement for preserving it in the state one regards as suitable for it? One can think in that way about something that goes on essentially unchanged from the point at which it was when it started. That will not do for the body social. Its life is a continual changing of each thing that arises in it. To fix on some form as the best, and expect it to remain in that form, is to undermine the very conditions of its life.

One of the requisites for the life of the social organism is that, as already stated, those who can serve the community through their individual abilities should not lose the possibility of doing so on their own initiative. This includes independent use of the means of production. I shall not use the common argument that the prospect of the gains associated with the means of production is needed as a stimulus. The concept presented here, of a progressive evolution in social conditions, must lead to the expectation that this kind of stimulus to social activity can drop away. This result can come through the setting free of the spiritual life from the political and the economic social entities.

The liberated spiritual life will of itself inevitably evolve a social sense, and out of this will arise stimuli of quite a different sort from those that lie in the hope of economic advantage. The question here is not so much concerned with the kind of impulse that makes men like private ownership of the means of production. We must ask whether the independent use of them, or use directed by the community, meets the requirements for the life of the social organism. We cannot here draw conclusions from conditions supposed to be found in primitive communities, but only from what corresponds to man's present stage of development.

At this present stage, the fruitful exercise of individual ability through the use of capital cannot make itself felt in the economic life unless the access to it is free and independent. Where there is to be fruitful production, this access must be possible, not because it will bring advantage to an individual or group but because, directed by a social sense, such use of the means of production is the best way of serving the community.

Man is connected with what he (alone or with others) is producing, as he is connected with the skill of his own arms and legs. Interfering with this free access to the means of production is like crippling the free exercise of bodily skill.

Private ownership is simply the means of providing this free and independent use of the means of production. As far as the body social is concerned, the only significance of ownership is that the owner has the right to use his property on his own free initiative. One sees, joined together in the life of society, two things of quite different significance for the social organism. There is the free access to the capital basis of social production, and on the other hand there is the rights relationship that arises between the user and other people. This comes up through the fact that his right of use keeps these other people from any free activity on the basis of this same capital.

It is not the original free use that leads to social harm but the continuance of the right of use after the conditions that tied it to his individual abilities have come to an end. One who sees the social organism as something growing, developing, cannot fail to understand what is meant. For what is living, there exists no fruitful arrangement by which a finished process does not later, in its turn, become detrimental. The question is entirely one of intervening at the right moment, when what had been opportune and helpful is beginning to become detrimental.

There must be the possibility of the free access of individual capacities to the capital-basis. It must also be possible to change the right of ownership connected with it in the moment that this right starts to change into a means for the unjust acquisition of power. There is an institution, introduced in our times, that meets this social requirement, but only partially since it applies simply to "spiritual property." I refer to copyrights. Such property, after the author is dead, passes after a certain length of time into the ownership of the community, for free use. Here we have an underlying conception that accords with the actual nature of life in a human society. Closely as the production of a purely spiritual (cultural) possession is bound up with the gifts and capacities of the individual, it is at the same time a result of the common social life and must pass, at the right moment, back into this. It is just the same with other property. By the aid of his property the individual produces for the service of the community, but this is only possible in cooperation with the community. Accordingly, the right to the use of a piece of property cannot be exercised separately from the interests of the community. The problem is not how to abolish ownership of the capital-basis, but how this ownership can be so administered that it serves the community in the best way possible.

The way to do this can be found in the Threefold Order of Society. The people united in the social organism act as a totality through the rights state. The exercise of individual abilities comes under the spiritual organization.

Everything in the body social, viewed from a sense of actualities (and not from subjective opinions and theories), indicates the necessity for the threefolding of this organism. This is especially clear as regards the relation of individual abilities to the capital-basis and its ownership. The rights state will not interfere with the formation and control of private property in capital so long as the connection of this with personal ability remains such that the private control represents a service to the whole social organism. Moreover, it will remain a rights state in its dealings with private property. It will never, itself, take over the ownership of private property. It will only bring it about that the right of use is transferred at the proper moment to a person, or group of persons, who are, again, capable of establishing a relation to this ownership that is based on individual abilities. This will benefit the body social in two quite different ways. The democratic foundation of the rights state being concerned with what touches all men equally, there will be a watch kept to see that property rights do not in the course of time become property wrongs. The other benefit is that the individual human abilities into whose control the property is given (since the state itself does not administer property), are thus furnished the means of fructifying the whole social organism.

Under an organization of this sort, property rights, or their exercise, can be left attached to a personality for as long as seems opportune. One can conceive the representatives of the rights state as laying down quite different laws at different times concerning the transfer of property from one person or group to another. Today, when all private property has come to be regarded with great distrust, the proposal is to convert it wholesale into community property. If people go far on this road they will see that they are strangling the life of the social organism and, taught by experience, they will then pursue a different path. It would surely be better now, at this time, to take measures that would secure social health on the lines here indicated.

So long as an individual (alone or with a group) continues to carry on that productive activity that first procured him a capital-basis to work on, he shall retain the right to use accumulations arising as gains on the primary capital, if these are used for the productive extension of the business. As soon as this particular personality ceases to control the work of production, this accumulation of capital shall pass on to another person or group, to carry on the same kind of business or some other branch of productive industry useful to the whole community. Capital accumulating from a productive industry, that is not used for its extension, must from the beginning go the same way. Nothing shall count as the personal property of the individual directing the business except what he gets in accordance with the claims for compensation that he made when he first took over the business. These were claims he felt able to make on the ground of his personal abilities, and that appear justified by the fact that he was able to impress people sufficiently with his abilities for them to trust him with capital. If the capital has been increased through his personal exertions, then a portion of this increment will also pass into his private ownership—this addition to his original earnings representing a percentage of the increase of the capital. Where the original person controlling an industry is unable or unwilling to continue in charge, the capital used to start it will either pass over to the new person in charge (along with all its incumbent obligations), or will revert to the original owners, according to their decision.

In such an arrangement one is dealing with transfers of a right. The legal regulation of the terms of such transfers is a matter for the rights state. It will also be up to the rights state to see that these transfers are carried out and to administer them. It is conceivable that details of such regulations for transfers of a right will vary greatly in accordance with how the common sense of right (the rights-consciousness) varies in its view of what *is* right. No mode of conception, which, like this one, aims at being true to life, will ever attempt to do more than indicate the general direction that such regulation should take. Keeping to this direction and using one's understanding, one will always discover the appropriate thing to do in any concrete instance. One must always judge the right course according to the circumstances and from the spirit of the thing. For instance, it is obvious that the rights state must never use its control of rights-transfers to get any capital into its own hands. Its only business will be to see that the transfer is made to a person or group whose individual abilities seem to warrant it.

This way of thinking also presupposes, as a general rule, that anyone who has to undertake such a transfer of capital from his own hands will be free to select his successor in the use of it. He will be free to select a person or group, or else transfer the right of use to a corporate body of the spiritual organization. For anyone who has given practical services to society through his management of capital is likely, from native ability and social sense, to be able to judge what should be done with the capital afterwards. It will be more to the advantage of the community to abide by what he decides than to leave the decisions to people who have no direct connection with the matter.

Some settlement of this kind will be required in the case of capital accumulations over a certain amount, acquired through use of the means of production—and land also comes under this category. The exception is where the gains become private property by terms of the original agreement for the exercise of the individual's capacities.

In the latter case, what is so earned, as well as all savings coming from the results of a person's own work, will remain in the earner's private possession until his death, or in the possession of his descendants until some later date. Until this time, these savings will draw interest from any person who gets them to create means of production. The amount of interest will be the outcome of the general rights-consciousness and will be fixed by the rights state.

In a social order based on the principles described here it will be possible to draw a complete distinction between yields resulting from the employment of the means of production and sums accumulated through the earnings of personal labor, spiritual or physical. It accords with the common sense of right, as well as being to the general social interest, that these two things should be kept distinct. What a person saves and places at the disposal of a productive industry is a service in the interests of all, since this makes it possible for personal ability to direct production. Where, after the rightful interest has been deducted, there is an increase that arises out of the means of production, that increase is due to the collective working of the whole social organism. This must accordingly flow back into it again in the way described above. All that the rights state will have to do is to pass a resolution that these capital accumulations are to be transferred in the way prescribed.

The state will not decide which material or spiritual branch of production is to have the disposal of capital so transferred, or of capital savings. For it to do so would lead to the tyranny of the state over spiritual and material production. But anyone who does not want to select his successor to exercise the right of disposal over capital he has created, may appoint a corporate body of the spiritual sphere to do this.

Property acquired through saving, together with the interest on it, will also pass at the earner's death, or a little while later, to some person or group actively engaged in spiritual or material production, but it must only go to a producer; if it went to an unproductive person, it would simply become private income. The choice will be made by the earner in his last will. Here again, no person or group can be chosen direct; it will be a question of transferring the right of disposal to a corporation of the spiritual organism. Only when a person himself makes no disposition of his savings will the rights state act on his behalf and require the spiritual organization to dispose of them.

In a society ordered on these lines, due regard is paid both to the free initiative of the individual and to the social interests of the general community. In fact these are fully met through the setting free of private initiative to serve them. Whoever has to give his labor over to the direction of another person can know that under such an order of things their joint work will bear fruit to the best advantage of the community, and therefore to that of the worker himself.

The social order here conceived will establish a proportionate relation, satisfactory to healthy human feeling, between the prices of manufactured goods and the two joint factors of their production. These two factors are, as has been shown, human labor and the right of use over capital (embodied in the means of production), which are subject to the common sense of right.

No doubt all sorts of imperfections may be found in what is presented here. Imperfections, however, do not matter. The important thing, if we want to be true to life, is not to lay down a perfect and complete program for all time but to point out the direction for practical work. The special instances discussed here are simply intended as illustrations, to map out the direction more clearly. Any particular illustration may be improved upon, and this will be all to the good, provided the right direction is not lost.

The claims of general humanity and justified personal and family interests can be brought into harmony through social institutions of this kind. For instance, it may be pointed out that there will be a great temptation for people to transfer their property during their lifetime to their descendants or some one of them. It is quite easy to give such a person the appearance of a producer while in fact he may be quite incompetent as compared with others who would be much better in the place he holds. The temptation to do this can be reduced to a minimum: the rights state has only to require that property transferred from one member of a family to another must under all circumstances be made over to a corporation of the spiritual system after a certain period of time following the first owner's death. Or an evasion of the rule may be prevented in some other way by rights-law. The rights state will merely see to it that the property *is* made over in this fashion. The spiritual organization must make provision for the choice of the person to inherit it.

Through the fulfilling of these principles there will arise a general sense that the next generation must be trained and educated to fit them for the body social, and that one must not do social damage by passing capital on to non-productive persons. No one in whom a real social sense is awakened cares to have his own connection with the capital-basis of his work carried on by any individual or group whose personal abilities do not warrant it.

Nobody who has a sense for what is practicable will regard these proposals as utopian. For the kind of institutions here proposed are such as can grow directly out of existing circumstances anywhere in life. The only thing is that people will have to make up their minds to give up administering the spiritual life and industrial economy within the rights state. This includes not raising opposition when what should happen really happens—when, for instance, private schools and colleges are started, and the economy is put on its own footing. There is no need to abolish state schools and the state economic undertakings at once. Beginning perhaps in a small way, it will be found increasingly possible to do away with the whole structure of state education and state economy.

The first necessity is for people who are convinced of the correctness of these social ideas, or similar ones, to make it their business to spread them. If such ideas find understanding, they will arouse in people confidence in the possibility of a healthy transformation of present conditions into conditions that do not show the evils we see about us. Only out of this sort of confidence can a really healthy evolution come. To achieve such confidence one must be able to see clearly how new institutions can be connected with what exists at present. The essential feature of the ideas being developed here is that they do not propose to bring about a better future by destroying the present social order further than has already been done. Their realization builds on what already exists, and in the process brings about the falling away of what is unhealthy. A solution that does not establish confidence in this respect will fail to attain something that is absolutely necessary: a further evolution in which the values of the goods already transformed through human labor, and the human faculties men have developed, will not be cast away but be preserved.

Even a radical person can acquire confidence in a form of social reconstruction that includes the preservation of already accumulated values if he is introduced to ideas capable of initiating really sane and healthy developments. Even he will have to recognize that whatever social class gets into power, it will not be able to get rid of existing evils unless its impulses are supported by ideas that can put life and health into the body social. To despair because one cannot believe there will be enough people with understanding for these ideas—provided the ideas are spread with the necessary energy— would be to despair of human nature's capacity for taking up healthy and purposeful impulses. All one should ask is, what must be done to give full force to the teaching and spread of ideas that can awaken men's confidence?

The first obstacle will be in current habits of thought. It will be objected that any dismemberment of social life is inconceivable, that the three branches cannot be torn apart because, in actual practice, they are everywhere intertwined. Or else there will be the opinion that it is quite possible to give each of the branches its necessary independent character under the Onefold State, and thus these ideas are mere empty cobweb-spinning. The first objection comes from unreal thinking. Some people believe that unity of social life is only possible when it is brought about by law. The facts of life itself require just the opposite: that unity must be the result, the final outcome, of all the streams of activity flowing together from various directions. Recent developments have run counter to this principle and so men resisted the "order" brought about from outside. It is this that has led to present social conditions. The second prejudice (the idea that these things could be accomplished under the Onefold State) arises from the inability to distinguish the radical differences in the operation of the three organs of the body social. People do not see that man stands in a separate and peculiar relation to each of the three. They do not see that each of these relationships needs the chance to evolve its own form, apart from the other two, so that it may work together with them.

People think that if one sphere of life follows its own laws, then everything needed for life must come out of this one sphere. If, for example, economic life were regulated in such a way as to meet men's wants, then a proper rights life and spiritual life would spring out of this economic soil as well. Only unrealistic thinking could believe this to be possible. There is nothing whatever in economic life that provides any motive for guiding what runs through the relations of man to man and comes from the sense of right. If people insist on regulating this relationship by economic motives, the result will be that the human being, his labor and his control of the means of labor, will all be harnessed to the economic life. The economy will run like clockwork but man will be a wheel in this mechanism. Economic life has a tendency always to go in one direction, a direction that we must balance from another side. It is not a question of rights regulations following the course set by economic life, but rather, economic life should be constantly subject to the rules of right that concern man simply as man. In this way a human existence within the economy then becomes possible. Economic life itself can develop in a way beneficial to man only when individual ability grows on its own separate soil (detached from the economic system) and continuously conveys to it the forces that economics and industry themselves are powerless to produce.

It is a curious thing that in purely external matters people can readily see the advantage of a division of labor. They do not expect a tailor to keep a cow in order to get milk. When it comes to a recognition of the individual functions of the different spheres of human life, however, they think no good can come of anything but a onefold system.

* * *

It is clear that social ideas that are related to life as it really is, will stimulate objections from every side. Real life breeds contradictions, and anyone accepting this fact will work for social arrangements whose own contradictions will be balanced out by means of other arrangements. He dare not believe that an institution that is "ideally perfect" according to his thinking will involve no contradictions when it is realized in practice.

It is an entirely justified present-day demand that institutions in which production is carried on for the benefit of the individual be replaced by institutions in which production is carried on for the general consumption. Anyone who fully recognizes this demand will not be able to come to the conclusion of modern Socialism, that therefore the means of production must go over from private to common ownership. Indeed, he will be forced to a quite different conclusion, namely, that proper methods must be used to convey to the community what is privately produced by individual energy and capacity.

The tendency of the more recent economic impulses has been to obtain income by mass production. The aim of the future must be to find out, by means of economic Associations, the best production methods and distribution channels for the actual needs of consumption. The rights institutions will see that a productive industry does not remain tied up with any individual or group longer than personal ability warrants. Instead of common ownership, there will be a circulation of the means of production through the body social. This will constantly bring them into the hands of those whose individual ability can employ them best in the service of the community.

That same connection between personality and the means of production, which previously existed through private ownership, will thus be established for periods of time. For the head of a business and his assistants will have the means of production to thank for being able to earn, by their personal abilities, the income they asked. They will not fail to improve production as far as is possible, since every improvement brings them, not indeed the whole profit, but nevertheless a portion of the added returns. For profits, as shown above, go to the community only to the extent of what is left over after deducting the percentage due to the producer for improvements in production. It is in the spirit of the whole thing that if production falls off, the producer's income must diminish in the same proportion in which it rises with increased production, but at all times the manager's income will come out of the spiritual work he has done. It will not come out of the profits that are based on the interplay of forces at work in the life of the community.

One can see that with the realization of social ideas such as these, institutions that already exist will acquire an altogether new significance. Property ceases to be what it has been up until now, and it will not be forced back to an obsolete form, such as that of communal ownership. It is, rather, taken forward, to become something quite new. The objects of ownership will be brought into the stream of social life. The individual cannot, motivated by his private interests, control them to the injury of the general public. Neither can the general public control them bureaucratically to the injury of the individual. It is rather that the qualified individual will have access to them as a means of serving the public.

A sense for the general public interest will have a chance to develop when social impulses of this sort are realized, with approaches that place production on a sound basis and safeguard the social organism from the danger of sudden (economic) crises. Also, an Administrative Body occupied solely with the processes of economic life, will be able to bring these back into balance when this appears to be necessary. Suppose, for instance, that a concern were not in a position to pay its creditors the interest due them on their invested personal savings. Then, if the firm is nevertheless recognized as meeting a need, it will be possible to get other business concerns, by free agreement, to make up the shortage in what is due to these investors.

A self-contained economic life that gets its rights basis from outside, and is supplied from without by a constant flow of fresh human ability as it comes on the scene, will, itself, have to do only with economic matters. Through this fact it will be able to facilitate a distribution of goods that procures for everyone what he can rightfully have in relation to the general state of prosperity of the community. If one person seemingly has more income than another, this will only be because this "more" resulting from the individual's talents benefits the general public.

* * *

In a social organism that shapes itself in the light of these conceptions, the taxes needed for the rights life can be regulated through agreement between the leaders of the rights life and those of the economic life. Everything needed for the maintenance of the cultural-spiritual life will come as remuneration resulting from voluntary appreciation on the part of individuals active in the body social. This spiritual life rests on a healthy basis of individual initiative, exercised in free competition among the private individuals suited to spiritual-cultural work.

Only in the kind of social organism meant here will the rights administration develop the necessary understanding for administering a just distribution of goods. In an economic life that does not have the claim on men's labor prescribed by the single branches of production, but rather has to carry on business with the amount of labor power the rights-law allows it, the value of goods will be determined by what men actually put into it in the way of work. It will not allow the work men do to be determined by the goods-values, into the formation of which human welfare and human dignity do not enter. Such a social organism will keep in view rights that arise from purely human conditions.

Children will have the right to education. The father of a family will be able to have a higher income as a worker than the single man. The "more" that he gets will come to him through agreement among all three branches of the body social. Such arrangements could meet the right to education in the following way. The administration of the economic organization estimates the amount of revenue that can be given to education, in line with general economic conditions, and the rights state determines the rights of the individual in this regard, in accord with the opinion of the spiritual organization. Here again, since we are thinking in line with reality, this instance is merely intended to indicate the direction in which such arrangements can go. It is quite possible that for a specific instance quite other arrangements may be found to be the right thing. In any case, this "right thing" will only be found through the working together of all three independent members of the social organism. For the purposes of this presentation, our concern is merely to discover the really practical thing— unlike so much that passes for practical today. We refer to such a membering of the social organism as shall give people the basis on which to bring about what is socially useful.

On a par with the right of children to education is the right of the aged, of invalids and widows to a maintenance. The capital basis for this will flow to it through the circulatory system of the social organism in much the same way as the capital contributed for the education of those who are not yet capable of working. The essential point in all this is that the income received by anyone who is not personally an earner should not be determined by the economic life. Rather should it be the other way round: the economic life must be dependent on what develops in this respect out of the rights consciousness. The people working in an economic organism will have so much the less from what is produced through their labor, the more that has to go to the non-earners. Only, this "less" will be borne fairly by all the members of the body social when the social impulses meant here are really put into practice. The education and the support of those who cannot work, concerns all mankind in common. Under a rights state, detached from economic life, it will become the common concern in actual practice. For in the rights state there works what in every grown human being must have a voice.

A social organism so arranged will bring the surplus that a person produces as a result of his individual capacities into the general community. It will do it in just the same way as it takes from the general community the just amount needed for the support of those less capable. "Surplus value" will not be created for the unjustified enjoyment of the individual, but for the enhancement of what can give wealth of soul and body to the whole social organism, and to foster whatever is born of this organism even though it is not of immediate service to it.

Someone might incline to the thought that the careful separation of the three members of the body social only has a value in the realm of ideas (ideal value), and that it would come about "by itself" under a onefold state or under a cooperative economic society that includes the state and rests on communal ownership of the means of production. He should, however, consider the special sorts of social institutions that must come into being if the three-folding is made a reality. For instance, the political government will no longer have to recognize the money as a legal medium of exchange. Money will, rather, owe its recognition to the measures taken by the various administrative bodies within the economic organization. For money, in a healthy social organism, can be nothing but an order for commodities that other people have produced and that one can draw out of the total economic life because of the commodities that one has oneself produced and given over to this sphere. It is the circulation of money that makes a sphere of economic activity into an economic unit. Everyone produces, on the roundabout path of the whole economic life, for everyone else.

Within the economic sphere one is concerned only with economic values. Within this sphere, the deeds that arise out of the spiritual and the state spheres also take on the character of a commodity. What a teacher does for his pupil is, for the economic circuit, a commodity. The teacher's individual ability is no more paid for than is the worker's labor-power. All that can possibly be paid for in either case is what, proceeding from them, can pass as a commodity or commodities into the economic circuit. How free initiative, and how rights, must act so that the commodity can come into being, lies as much outside the economic circuit itself as does the action of the forces of nature on the grain crop in a bountiful or a barren year. For the economic circuit, both the spiritual sphere—as regards its claim on economic returns—and the state, are simply producers of commodities. Only, what they produce is not a commodity within their own spheres. It first becomes one when it is taken up into the economic circuit.

The purely economic value of a commodity (or an accomplishment), as far as it is expressed in money terms, will depend on the efficiency, in the economic organism, that is developed by the management of the economy. On the measures taken by management, will depend the progress of economic life—always on the basis of the spiritual and the rights foundation developed by those other members of the social organism. The money-value of a commodity will then indicate that the economic organization is producing the commodity in a quantity corresponding to the demand for it. If the premises laid down in this book are realized, then the body economic will not be dominated by the impulse to amass wealth through sheer quantity of production. Rather will the production of goods adapt itself to the wants, through the agency of the Associations that will spring up in all manner of connections. In this way the proportion, corresponding in each case to the actual demand, will become established between the money-value of an article and the arrangements made in the body social for producing it.*

In the healthy society, money will really be nothing but a measure of value, since behind every coin or bill there stands the tangible piece of production, on the strength of which alone the owner of the money could acquire it. The nature of these conditions will necessarily bring about arrangements that will deprive money of its value for its possessor when once it has lost the significance just pointed out. Arrangements of this sort have already been alluded to. Money property passes back, after a fixed period, into the common pool, in whatever the proper form may be. To prevent money that is not working in industry from being held back by its possessors through evasion of the provisions made by the economic organ-

---

* *Author's Note.* A sound proportion between the prices of the various goods produced can only be achieved in economic life as an outcome of a social administration that springs up in this way from the free cooperation of the three branches of the body social. The proportion between prices of various goods must be such that anyone working receives as counter-value for what he has produced as much as is necessary to satisfy his total wants and the wants of his dependents until he has again turned out a product requiring the equivalent labor. It is impossible to fix such a price relation officially in advance. It must come as the result of the living cooperation between the Associations actively at work in the body social. Prices will however certainly settle down into such a normal relationship, provided the joint work of the Associations rests on a healthy cooperation between the three members of the social organization. It must develop with the same sureness that a safe bridge must come into being when it is built according to the proper laws of mathematics and mechanics. It may be said that social life does not invariably obey its own laws, like a bridge. No one, however, will make this objection who is able to recognize that it is primarily the laws of life and not those of mathematics that, throughout this book, are conceived as underlying social life.

ization, there can be a new coinage, or new printing of bills, from time to time. One result of this will no doubt be that the interest derived from any capital sum will gradually diminish. Money will wear out, just as commodities wear out. Nevertheless, such a measure will be a right and just one for the state to enact.

There can be no compound interest. If a person puts aside savings, he has certainly rendered past services that gave him a claim on future counter-service in terms of commodities. This is in the same way as present services claim present services in exchange. Nevertheless, his claims cannot go beyond a certain limit. For claims that date from the past require the productions of labor in the present to satisfy them. Such claims must not be turned into a means of economic coercion. The practical realization of these principles will put the problem of the currency standard on a sound basis. For no matter what form money may take owing to other conditions, its standard will lie in the intelligent arrangement of the whole economic body through its administration. The problems of safeguarding the currency standard will never be satisfactorily solved by any state by means of laws. Present governments will only solve it when they give up attempting the solution on their own account and leave the economic organism—which will have been detached from the state—to do what is needful.

*　*　*

There is a lot of talk about the modern division of labor in connection with its results in time-saving, in perfecting the manufacture and facilitating the exchange of commodities. Little attention is paid to its effect on the relation of the human individual to his work. Nobody working in a social organism based on the division of labor really earns his income himself. He earns it through the work of all those who have a part in the social organism. A tailor who makes a coat for his own use does not have the same relationship to it as does a person who, under primitive conditions, still has all the other necessities of life to provide for himself. The tailor makes the coat in order to enable him to make clothing for other people, and its value for him depends entirely on what other people produce. The coat is really a means of production. Many people will say this is hair-splitting. They won't say this when they come to consider the formation of values in the economic process. Then they will see that in an economic organism based on the division of labor one simply cannot work for oneself. All a person can do is work for others and let others work for him. One can as little work for oneself as one can eat oneself up. One can, however, establish arrangements that are in direct opposition to the very essence of the division of labor. That happens when the production of goods only takes place in order to transfer to the individual as private property what he can only produce because of his place in the social organism.

The division of labor makes for a social organism in which the individual lives in accordance with the conditions of the whole body of the organism. Economically it precludes egoism. If, then, egoism nevertheless persists in the form of class privileges and the like, a condition of social instability sets in, leading to disturbances in the social organism. We are living under such conditions today. There may be people who think it futile to insist that rights conditions and other things must bring themselves into line with the non-egoistic production resulting from the division of labor. Such a person may as well conclude, from his own premises, that one cannot do anything at all, that the social movement can lead nowhere. As regards the social movement, one can certainly do no good unless one is willing to give reality its due. It is inherent in the mode of thought underlying what is written here, that man's activities within the body social must be in line with the conditions of its organic life.

*   *   *

Anyone who is only capable of forming his ideas by the system he is accustomed to, will be uneasy when he is told that the relation between the employer (work director) and the worker is to be separated from the economic organism. For he will believe that such a separation is bound to lead to the depreciation of money and a return to primitive conditions of industrial economy. (Dr. Rathenau takes this view in his book, *After the Flood*, and from his standpoint it is a defensible one.) This danger is, however, counteracted by the threefolding of the social organism.

The autonomous economic organism, working jointly with the rights organism, completely detaches the money relationships from the labor conditions, which rest on the rights laws. The rights conditions cannot have any direct influence on money conditions, for these latter are the result of the administration of the economic organism. The rights relationship between employer and worker will not one-sidedly show itself in money values at all. For with the elimination of wages, which represent a relation of exchange between commodities and labor, money value remains simply a measure of the value of one commodity, or piece of work, as against another. If one studies the effects of the threefolding upon the social organism, one will become convinced that it will lead to institutions that do not as yet exist in the forms of the state as we have experienced them up to now.

These arrangements can be swept clear of all that today is felt as class struggle, for this struggle is based on the wages of labor being tied up in the economic processes. Here, we are describing a form of the social organism in which the concept of the wages of labor undergoes a transformation, no less than does the old concept of property. Through this transformation there is created a social relationship between human beings that is vital, is related to life.

Only a superficial judgment would find that these proposals amount in practice merely to converting hourly wages into piece wages. One might be led to this conclusion by a one-sided view of the matter, but this one-sided view is not what we are considering here. Rather, the point is the elimination of the wage-relation altogether and its replacement by a share-relation (based on contract) between employer and workers. We approach this in terms of its connection with the whole organization of the body social. It may seem to a person that the portion of the product of labor that falls to the worker is a piece wage. This is because one fails to see that this "piece wage," which is not a "wage" at all, finds expression in the value of the product. Furthermore, it does so in a way that puts the worker in a position with relation to other members of the social organism that is quite different from the one that arose out of class supremacy based one-sidedly on economic factors. Therewith, the demand for elimination of the class struggle is satisfied.

To those who hold the theory (heard also in Socialist circles) that evolution must bring the solution of the social question and that it is impossible to present views and say they ought to be realized, we must reply: Certainly evolution will bring about what must be, but in the social organism men's idea-impulses are realities. When time has moved on a little and what today can only be thought, can be realized, then this will be present in the evolution. If one waits until then, it will be too late to accomplish certain things that are required now by today's facts. It is not possible to observe evolution in the social organism objectively, from outside, as one does in nature. One must bring about the evolution. That is why views bent on "proving" social requirements as one "proves" something in natural science are so disastrous for healthy social thinking. A "proof" in social matters can only exist if it takes into account not only what is existing but also what is present in human impulses like a seed (often unknown to the people themselves) that will realize itself.

* * *

One of the ways in which the threefolding of the social organism will prove that it is founded on what is essential in human social life will be the removal of the judicial function from the sphere of the state. It will be up to the state institutions to determine the rights that are to be observed between individuals or groups of men. The passing of judgment, however, is the function of institutions developed out of the spiritual organization. In passing judgment, a great deal depends on the opportunity the judge has for perceiving and understanding the particular circumstances of the person he is trying. Nothing can assure this except those ties of trust and confidence that draw men together in the institutions of the spiritual sphere. These must be the main consideration in setting up the courts of law.

Possibly the administration of the spiritual organization might nominate a panel of judges who could be drawn from the widest range of spiritual professions and would return to their own calling at the expiration of a certain period. Within definite limits, everybody would then have the opportunity of selecting a particular person on the panel for five or ten years. This would be someone in whom he feels sufficient confidence to be willing to accept his verdict in a civil or criminal suit, if it should come to that. There would always be enough judges in the neighborhood where anyone was living, to give significance to this power of choice. A complainant would always have to apply to the defendant's judge.

Only consider the importance such an institution would have had for the territories of Austria-Hungary. In districts of mixed language, the member of any nationality would have been able to choose a judge of his own people. Apart from nationality, there are many fields of life where such an arrangement can be of benefit to healthy development.

For more detailed acquaintance with points of law, the judges and courts will have the help of officials (also selected by the spiritual administration) who will, however, not themselves decide cases. The same administration will also have to set up courts of appeal. The kind of life that will go on in society through a realization in practice of the conditions we are presuming here will bring it about that a judge is in touch with the life and feelings of the ones brought before him. His own life—outside the brief period of his judgeship—will make him familiar with their lives and the circles they move in. The social sense developed in such a society will also show in the judicial activity.

The carrying out of a sentence is the affair of the rights state.

*   *   *

It is not necessary at this time to go into arrangements that will be necessitated in other fields of life by the realization of what has been presented here. This would obviously take up unlimited space.

The instances of social arrangements given here make clear that this is not an attempt to revive the three old "estates" of the Plough, the Sword and the Book. The intention is the very opposite of such a division into classes. It is the social organism itself that will be functionally membered, and just through this fact man will be able to be truly man. He himself will have his own life's roots in each of the three members. He will have a practical footing in that member in which he stands by way of occupation. His relation to the other two will be actual and living, developing out of his connection with their institutions. Threefold will be the social organism as apart from man, forming the groundwork of his life, and each man as a man will unite the three members.

CHAPTER IV

INTERNATIONAL ASPECTS

The internal structure of a healthy social organism makes its international relations also threefold. Each of the three spheres will have its own independent relations with the corresponding sphere of the other social organisms elsewhere. Economic relationships between countries will arise without the relations between their rights-states having a direct influence upon them.* Conversely, the relations between their rights-states will, within certain limits, develop in complete independence of their economic connections. This independence of origin will enable these two sets of relationships to act as a check upon each other in cases of disputes. Such a close interweaving of interests between the individual social organ-

---

* *Author's Note:* It may be urged that the rights relations and the economic relations form one indivisible whole in actual reality. This, however, misses the point of what is meant by the threefold membering. Of course, in the mutual intercourse and exchange, taken as a total process, the two different sets of relations (between the rights systems and the economic systems) work together as a single whole. But it is a different matter whether one makes rights regulations to suit the requirements of economic intercourse, or whether one first shapes them by the common sense of right and then lets the result of this affect the economic process.

isms will develop as will make territorial frontiers seem negligible as far as real communities of human beings are concerned.

The spiritual organizations of the different countries will be able to enter into mutual relationships that stem only from the common spiritual life of mankind. Detached from the state and placed on its own footing, the spiritual life will develop all sorts of connections that are impossible when recognition of spiritual services rests with the state rather than with the administration of a spiritual body. In this regard, there is no difference between achievements of science, which are frankly international, and those of any other spiritual field.

The common language of a nation, and all that goes along with this, constitutes such a field of spiritual life. The national consciousness itself belongs in this field. The people of one language-area do not come into unnatural conflict with those of another, so long as they do not try to make their national culture predominant by the use of their state-organization or their economic power. If one national civilization spreads more readily and has greater spiritual fertility than another, then it is quite right that it should spread. The process of spreading will be a peaceful one, provided it comes about solely through establishments of the spiritual organisms.

At present the keenest opposition to the threefolding of the social organism will come precisely from those groups that have developed out of the fact of their possessing a speech and national culture in common. Such opposition will, however, collapse because of the common goal, of which all mankind will have to become increasingly conscious just out of the very necessities of modern life. Mankind will come to feel that each of its parts can only lead a life worthy of their common humanity by uniting in a vital manner

78

with all the other parts. National affinities, along with other natural impulses, are among the causes that led to the historical development of communities in rights and of economic communities. But the forces through which nationalities grow require free mutual interaction that is not hindered by any relationships that develop between the States and the Economic Associations. This will be achieved if the various nations bring about the internal threefolding of their own body social in such a way that every one of the three branches can develop its independent relations to the other social organisms.

In this way people, states and economic bodies become interrelated in formations that are extremely varied in shape and character. These link every part of mankind with every other part, in such a way that each is conscious of the life of the others pulsing through its own daily interests. A League of Nations comes into being out of basic impulses that correspond to actual realities. There will be no need to "institute" one based on one-sided legal theories of right.*

An important thing, in terms of the realities, is that while the social aims presented here have value for mankind as a whole, they can be put into practice by any single social organism no matter what the attitude of other countries may at first be. If one country shapes itself into the three natural spheres, the representatives of these can enter international relations as a single body to deal with others, even if these are not yet ready to adopt the Threefold Order themselves. Whoever leads the way with the Threefold Order will

* *Author's Note.* Whoever thinks such things are "Utopias" fails to see that actual life is really struggling toward the very kind of arrangement that seems to them so utopian, and that the mischief going on in real life is due precisely to the fact that these arrangements are nowhere to be found.

be furthering a common goal of all mankind. What has to be done will come to pass far more through the strength produced by an aim that is rooted in actual human impulses than by way of diplomatic agreements or schemes drafted at conferences. This aim is conceived in thought on a basis of reality and is to be pursued in all the activities of life.

Any observer of the peoples and states during recent decades could see how the historically-developed state-structures, with their blending of spiritual, rights and economic life, were becoming involved in international relations that were leading to a catastrophe. At the same time it was equally plain to see that opposite forces, working in mankind's unconscious impulses, were tending towards the Threefold Order. It will be the remedy for those convulsions that have been brought about by the mania for unification. The "leaders of mankind," however, were not able to see what had for years been slowly developing. In the spring and early summer of 1914 one still found "statesmen" saying that thanks to the exertions of the governments, the peace of Europe was, as far as could be humanly foreseen, assured.

These "statesmen" simply had not the faintest notion that all they were doing and saying had absolutely lost touch with the course of real events. Yet these were the people who were looked up to as "practical." Whoever, during those last decades, developed ideas contrary to those of the "statesmen" was regarded as a "crank." I refer to ideas such as those expressed by the author of this book months before the war-catastrophe, speaking to a small audience in Vienna—a large audience would certainly have laughed him down. He spoke of the danger in more or less these words:

"The tendencies prevailing in present-day life will go on gathering strength until they end by annihilating themselves. One who looks at social life with the eyes of the spirit can see everywhere, the ghastly signs of social tumors forming. Here is the great menace to civilization, apparent to anyone who looks below the surface of existence. This is what is so terrible, so depressing. In fact, even if one were able to repress all interest in obtaining knowledge of life's events by means of a science recognizing the spirit, these signs alone would impel one to speak of the means of healing in words forceful enough to arouse the world. If the body social goes on developing as it has, it will become full of cultural sores that will be for it what cancers are in man's natural body."

Over the surface of these subterranean currents, which they could not and would not see, the ruling circles undertook measures they should not have taken; never any that would have established confidence between the various human communities.

Anyone who thinks that the social needs of the time played no part in causing the present world-catastrophe should consider what direction political impulses would have taken in the states that were rushing into war, if the meeting of these social needs had been included among the aims of the "statesmen." How much less inflammable material would have been piled up if people had, instead, worked at meeting these social needs.

It was the onefold form of the state, which the leaders were determined to preserve, that ran counter to healthy relations between the peoples.

If the independent spiritual life could have evolved beyond the frontiers of Austria and Serbia in a fashion that harmonized with the goals of these peoples, then this conflict (rooted in the spiritual life) need not have burst into a political catastrophe. Yet the habits of thought of the "statesmanlike" thinkers in Austria-Hungary could not conceive of state boundaries not coinciding with national cultural communities. They could not understand how spiritual organizations could be formed that would cut across state frontiers and form the school system and other branches of spiritual life. Yet this "inconceivable" thing is what international life demands in the new age.

What about the German Empire? It was founded at a time when modern demands for a healthy social organism were struggling for realization. To have accomplished this would have given the Empire a historical justification for existence. Here lay the task for those who were at the head of its affairs. Instead, they were satisfied with "social reforms" arising out of day to day needs. The state-structure they had in mind could only rest on military force. The one demanded by modern history would have had to rest on the realization of the impulses for a healthy social organism. German policy had, in 1914, reached a dead point and was bound, from sheer lack of inner content, to collapse like the proverbial "house of cards."

What has now resulted from the war-catastrophe has created a new situation. It is possible for the social impulses of mankind to influence this new situation in the sense conceived in this book. These social impulses should arouse a sense of responsibility throughout the civilized world. Some countries were able to stand aloof from the points at issue in 1914. From the social movement they cannot stand aloof. This is a question that admits of no political adversaries and no neutrals. Here there must be one human race working at one common task, willing to read the signs of the times and to act in accordance with them.